CW01372081

THE LETTERS OF
CARYLL HOUSELANDER

THE LETTERS OF
CARYLL HOUSELANDER

Edited by Maisie Ward

ଔ ଓ

CLUNY
Providence, Rhode Island

CLUNY MEDIA EDITION, 2023

This Cluny edition is a republication of *The Letters of Caryll Houselander: Her Spiritual Legacy*, originally published by Sheed & Ward in 1965.

For more information regarding this title
or any other Cluny Media publication,
please write to info@clunymedia.com, or to
Cluny Media, P.O. Box 1664, Providence, RI 02901

VISIT US ONLINE AT WWW.CLUNYMEDIA.COM

Cluny edition copyright © 2023 Cluny Media LLC

All rights reserved.

ISBN: 978-1685952013

Cover design by Clarke & Clarke
Cover image: Samuel John Peploe, *Pink Roses, Chinese Vase*,
1916, oil on canvas
Courtesy of Wikimedia Commons

CONTENTS

	Introduction	i
I.	To Mr. St. George	3
II.	To Elizabeth Billaux	7
III.	To Baroness Bosch van Drakestein	19
IV.	To a Correspondent Who Had Sent Her a Cry for Help	31
V.	To Archie Campbell-Murdoch	33
VI.	A Note on Incompatibility in Marriage	55
VII.	To Henry Tayler	59
VIII.	To a Friend about to Have an Illegitimate Baby	81
IX.	To Christine Spender	84
X.	To a Young Friend Who Married and Settled Abroad	96
XI.	To Mrs. Boardman	113
XII.	To a Friend with a Nervous Illness	165
XIII.	A Note on Repentance	184
XIV.	A Note on Friendship	186
XV.	To Lucile Hasley	189

INTRODUCTION

1. *The Impact of Caryll*

The biography of Caryll Houselander, wrote a friend, would surely further religious unity—and it was under the heading "A Christian Heroine" that the *Church Times* reviewed it, calling her "one of the greatest of the modern heroines of the Church of God." The Salvation Army's periodical *The Officer* felt that even if "Caryll Houselander might not square with a rigid nonconformist conscience...she had a mystical experience of God, a practical charity and an utter selflessness which we could well covet, and many officers would broaden their minds and deepen their love by reading this biography."

The sense of significant encounter dominated a great mass of private letters. "The impact of Caryll through the book is tremendous," wrote one. Another—"I found myself with tears in my heart and in my eyes." And a third—"If ever there was a soul who *shouts* to our neurotic age, it was she."

It looks indecent, I feel, for me as author to assemble these instances of a mail such as no earlier book of mine called forth, but, as Katherine Burton remarked, *Caryll Houselander* is the "biography of an autobiography": Caryll's own words, set in the framework of her life and thus brought home more vividly, are what have so profoundly affected *her* readers. "Surely your book is terribly important," wrote one, "even more so than a radio bringing us the music of the orchestra.… Having read [it] I will never again look at the river which flows beneath our flat and wish that less of the [town] sewage emptied into it so that I could throw myself into it and drown decently."

I gave the book to one group of lay men and women going through a singular trial of external pressure almost amounting to persecution and of consequent strains within the group. One of their best-loved members was dying of a painful cancer. All met Caryll by reading it, the dying woman turning to her "rhythms" for spiritual help, others seeing, if only in flashes, Caryll's own vision of Christ in all men, including especially their enemies.

But what makes the letters and reviews more interesting is the obvious possibility and occasional expression of a very different feeling. "Many readers," said one reviewer, "will have to line up with the devil's advocate. Facts are facts and there are many contradictions in the character of Caryll Houselander."

There are indeed, and I agree with Father Martindale, who began what was perhaps the last review he ever wrote:

> The author of this record forces a reader to find before his mind—to use, manipulate, or reject the words "sentimentalism, eccentricity, introversion, self-immolation, hysteria, neurosis, deliberate perversity or unconscious abnormality, extreme self-sacrifice (i.e., apostolic charity), heroism, mysticism, a rather crude sense of humour, a fundamental granite commonsense." If anyone fastened on one such he might be forgiven, but not justified.

Father Martindale cried out for a yet closer study of "this (to me) unique personality…not that anyone who wants the 'conventional' will get it, or who is alarmed by *intensity* of spiritual or psychological life would be pacified. But he might find a lot of fun in Caryll's experiences, as she did."

From private letters as well as reviews one fact emerged overwhelmingly. It *was* the unconventional in Caryll, the lack of plaster in her sainthood, which made its appeal to a Catholic community weary of the pattern and to those outside already suspicious of it.

Yet the pattern remains in Catholic circles so terribly pervasive that even those suspicious of it are still clinging to it. I found it curiously significant that the same friend who feared I should make Caryll look "sanctimonious" entreated me almost passionately not to mention her girlhood's love affair lest it should upset "her simple admirers." I doubt if people are ever as simple as all that. "Saints too," wrote one reader obviously comforted by the thought, "can have every physical and mental failing." "The real person," one young woman wrote, "is so much more real than she appeared in the books.... I rather felt she was almost inhumanly holy, and had never had a love affair, nor would ever touch gin!! I found the weaknesses make her so much stronger." A nurse from the heart of the Australian bush wrote, feeling that through Caryll she could bring strength to the many lonely souls who relied on her visits for spiritual as well as medical help, "In Caryll I think my own salvation lies." "Reading her life," wrote a man who had been through many trials, "was like drinking deeply of a good wine. It warmed and enlivened me"; while an aged nun wrote: "Caryll tried to live Christianity...with an intensity the reading of which left me weak at times."

"The book," ran another letter, "arrived at a time when I was down in the depths about myself. I have strong spiritual feelings of a vocation but don't know in which direction, also I had been told that no one could be a saint who smoked like I do nor exaggerated like I do nor one who was 'frivolous.' Consequently I was beginning to think I was unbalanced even to think of a vocation before all the above 'faults' were eradicated. You can imagine how your book gave me new heart and courage to start again and also to keep my own character and not be too influenced by others' opinions."

Most interesting, perhaps, of all the encounters with Caryll has been that of religious—both men and women. For, as one nun remarked: "She had no great devotion to religious women. What her ardent nature needed was freedom to do what needed to be done." Indeed I fancy that the words "holy" and "rule" appeared to Caryll sharply contrasted, and it is remarkable that those who see them as a harmony whereby to live should also treasure the experience of meeting this fierce critic and sceptic. Nun after nun wrote in reviews or private letters what Sister Maris Stella summed up in *The Commonweal*:

> Was Caryll Houselander a saint? Certainly not a conventional one. She was difficult. She seems to have preferred sinners to pious people. She was foolish about an old cat named Jones (for which this reviewer loves her). She had a critical tongue and a tendency to make quick, sometimes hard judgments. She often said what she later regretted. But she was able to be sorry— deeply and humbly so. And it was, above all, her nature to love; love was her life, and she gave it generously.

II. *The Letters*

Monsignor Knox wished that Caryll Houselander would establish a school of spirituality: the first letter printed below gives the central doctrine from which all the teaching in that school would have stemmed. The friend who sent it to me headed it with the words in which Caryll identified men and women she had met, "Unconscious Christs"—the discovery of the unknown Christ in man, by men in whom also He secretly dwells, was the chief achievement of her own spiritual life, the chief adventure in which she tried to engage all who came to her for help. This adventure must of its nature be integrated in our daily life: not alone with God on a mountain-top but looking for Him in the crowded streets, discovering Him among those unaware of His presence: "I was hungry and you gave me to eat." "When, Lord, did we see you hungry?"

But in making a selection from the letters sent me it has seemed desirable to include some which are not directly letters of advice but which cast light on her mental and spiritual growth and, in depicting her own life and activities, make her advice more valuable.

Reading recently a French collection of spiritual letters, I wondered why I found them so spiritless. Presently I realized that they were written as though from and to someone living in a vacuum. Other people, daily events and surroundings were ignored: one bodiless spirit was trying to lead another to the God who had not created them bodiless. There is nothing to show that God had set this man and woman, priest and nun, in a world of people—people to be thought about, to be helped, to be made helpful, whose hands could be clasped in a fellowship intended by Him to lead men to Him as what St. Thomas More might have called a merry company.

From the time that Caryll Houselander began to write even magazine articles her friends recognized a quality in her which led them to call on her for help—humour and profundity, humility and cheerful self-contempt, a touch of cynicism, and above all a realization that to give help always involves receiving it. Letters of spiritual advice often seem too much a one-way street. The giver will perhaps utter vague phrases about un-worthiness, but he seldom enough explains *why* he is unworthy or, most important of all, how his failures can be of value in helping another to conquer the same or similar difficulties. "Nous ne sommes pas plus forts les uns que les autres," said little Thérèse, and letters of self-revelation are often of the greatest value to other selves. But they need to be concrete and above all "real" in Newman's meaning when he distinguished real apprehension from merely notional.

And something else. We often wish in a volume of letters that we could see the other side of the correspondence. In these letters we almost do so. Caryll enters keenly into the actuality of each friend's life, she confides details about her own. These letters can be for the reader a real river of spiritual help formed by the junction of two streams. Writer and recipient have each contributed in their measure.

Caryll was beginning just after the First World War to discover amid hard work and much suffering that the Catholic religion can appeal to twentieth-century men and women as fully as to those of past ages if we will only show it to them—intellectually by knowing what it means and by being able to explain it; pictorially by the total commitment of our daily lives. To this period belong especially the conversion of her close friend Henry Tayler, and her letters about Catholicism to Elizabeth Billaux. Henry Tayler's pre-war 1939 letters have vanished, but I am including extracts from those of the war years to him and to the husband and wife, Sheila and Archie Campbell-Murdoch, who also both joined the Church through her.

The chief message of her life was probably to neurotics—a message of hope and cheer. She was certain she herself had never, technically speaking, been healed; but she had learnt to live with neurosis. It was a cross, but no more crippling a cross than, say, a broken leg. Bearing it as part of Christ's cross in the membership of His Mystical Body, she was able to share in His work of redemption. The neurotic had "an honourable place" in the Mystical Body.

This message was part of a larger whole. The world—at least our Western world—had appeared to be turning to God during the agonies of wartime. But she sensed with grief the revulsion immediately after—no, actually even before—the war's end. As she proposed a barefoot pilgrimage to Tyburn in reparation for the first dropping of the atom bomb ("I'm in deadly earnest," she wrote), she was realizing how far we had gone from the ideals uplifting the heart during the Battle of Britain.

But in hospital, awaiting her operation for the cancer that eventually killed her, she saw in the doctors and nurses the loving kindness of "other Christs," in the patients she found a marvellous community of suffering. And in London's largest mental home she found men and women praying in a little basement chapel, reaching out in their prayers to the whole world—and asking for themselves only a perfect abandonment to the will of God. She saw side by side "a visible close-up of what *is* happening in the world, but with all the masks and bandages off," an open vision of the problem of evil, but also "an unbelievable showing of the heart of the Mystical Body of Christ literally bleeding before God with the wounds of the world."

THE LETTERS OF
CARYLL HOUSELANDER

1

To Mr. St. George

I put this undated fragment first because it strikes so powerfully the keynote in Caryll's spiritual thought. It is all that remains of her correspondence with Mr. St. George. Sending it, he writes: "I first met Caryll Houselander when I was Honorary Secretary of the St. John Chrysostom Society many years ago. We were both interested in the problem of the Russian refugees. With her usual generosity she painted a Byzantine eight-pointed cross and gave it to the Society of St. John Chrysostom to be used when we organized the celebration of Liturgies according to the Russian Byzantine Rite in various Catholic churches in London in order that Catholics might become acquainted with the diversity of rites in the Catholic Church. Needless to say, she would not accept any payment for the cross, although she could ill afford not to do so."

… I have the deepest sympathy with the grief and anguish you suffer on account of the many inconsistencies in Western Christianity. I also experience bitter sorrow over them, not because I think myself better; on the contrary, consciousness of my own weakness and want of integrity has always made me long to find strength and example of something better in those Christians who *should* be examples, and go so far as to make examples of themselves.

I have been disappointed and often disheartened, but with the passing of time I have come to realize that just because Christ does go on living on earth in His Mystical Body, the circumstances of His historical life must and will continue all through time too. Thus among His chosen apostles there always will be inconsistencies; there always will be those who, even after living a long time with Him, ask, "Who is the greatest in the Kingdom of Heaven?"; and there always will be Pontius Pilates, condemning Him because to bow down before the humility and lowliness He stands for would cost them their prestige in the world; and there will always be Judases ready to sell Him. All this is part of His Passion going on now.

On the other hand, if His beauty seems at times almost hidden in what we see of Christians ("He hath no form nor comeliness, and when we see Him, there is no beauty that we should desire Him"), it is also revealed vividly over and over again where one least expects it in what I call "Unconscious Christs," and in people who are not considered respectable by the world.

I have a friend, a man who had an appalling tragedy in his life, namely that his wife went out of her mind and vanished with their four-year-old child. He spent a fortune trying to find them, but never did so. The police presumed that the poor woman had taken her life and the child's too, but the father never knew for certain, and does not know to this day. Well, he took to drink, which one can understand, and he went rapidly downhill until at last he was living in doss-houses and the streets.

He was in despair. He had lost faith in God and hope in life. He was drinking himself to death. Actually his kidneys were already diseased, and the doctors who had seen him in hospital told him to his face that he was a hopeless case. He just drank more to make an end of it all sooner.

Then for some time he disappeared. His occasional visits to me ceased. Five years passed in which all my efforts to trace him failed; and then to my astonishment he turned up again, a changed man. He no longer drank. He had got and kept a good job. He had taken a room and made it bright and homely although he was alone; and though he was still a semi-invalid he was able to work and was cheerful. No bitterness remained, only tenderness to everyone and belief in God.

What had happened? He told me that in the doss-houses the poor "down-and-outs," the "old lags" and the drunkards had shown him divine charity. When he was starving they had shared their last crusts with him. They had taught him to keep out the cold with old newspapers. They had spread their own ragged coats over him. They had shared with him the cigarette ends which they had picked up in the gutter.

He started to marvel. First of all he asked himself how was it that men so bad, so outcast, so insensitive and so ignorant as most of them really were, could have in them a strain of brotherly love stronger than the evil around them and sometimes in them? That was the question. But another one arose: What on earth could any of them see in *him* worth one moment's kindness?

He pondered this and arrived at the great truth of the presence of Christ in man. *Whatever is loving and whatever is lovable*, he thought, *is Christ in man.* This idea changed his whole life, as I have told you. The change, by the by, lasted. He has resumed his life among his fellow beings, but very often he returns to the doss-houses to try and give to others some of the faith and kindness they gave to him.

All that and much more is what I mean by the unconscious Christ in man; and to me it is this unconscious Christ which is the consolation for the unlovingness of the professionally righteous.

If you read again Our Lord's description of the Last Judgment, you will see that both the saved and the damned were astonished at the things attributed to them, as they did not do them with a *conscious* intention of Christhood. Their attitude is very unlike the awful system of spiritual double entry so dear to the hearts of nuns!

However, efforts at reform, even of some detail such as meaningless art, stupid education, etc., are useless—at least, that is what I feel. There are only two weapons against the worldly spirit which has possessed so many Catholics for so long, a worldly spirit that is not only unrecognized, but in some families regarded as a fine tradition! These two weapons are *Contemplation and visible, voluntary Poverty*, and these weapons I am certain have been forged already in Russia. I don't mean by the last remark that I am a Communist, but that out of the whole soul and experience and martyrdom of Russia, those weapons are already forged. But whether we shall take them into our hands and use them—that is another thing.

I think you agree with me that the failure of "Catholic Action" is that it takes a materialistic view of spiritual things. It strives for an *earthly* kingdom. This, however, seems the inevitable result of any big mass or group. A little study of psychology explains it easily, and I waste time in asserting it to you who know and feel it perhaps more acutely than I do myself.

Anyhow, what is more to the point is that from the hearts of such children as your little saint, Mary, the healing of the world begins; and there *are* a number of people who are learning the secret wonder of simplicity, humility and poverty. Everyone capable of thinking and of giving expression and reassurance to people drawn in that direction is a real saviour, and that certainly applies to you.

I have been thinking lately that it would be lovely if a contemplative Russian Order arose, and built a church or convent dedicated to the Holy Innocents. It is so astonishing that the very first martyrs were the little innocents slain by Herod as soon as Our Lord was born into the world. And it is true that whenever evil rises up and there are wars, etc., the first sufferers are innocent little children, as if the bright fire and perfection of children were something *essential* to the rebirth, to the renewing, and to the new forgiveness of Christ in the world, and in every heart in the world. *This rebirth is our one hope*, and that which makes me hope that it *will* happen is the great hosts of tiny little martyrs who have been killed in the war.

God does not take that sacrifice in vain. And surely Christ will be reborn, as small, naked and dependent on us as He was in Bethlehem. A lovely symbol of it would be a little church or monastery dedicated to the Holy Innocents, from which humility and the spirit of childhood should come back to mankind....

II

To Elizabeth Billaux (1935–1944)

Elizabeth Billaux is the wife of Louis Billaux. Caryll had worked for Louis' father, decorating churches, carving statues, etc. These letters were written partly to help Elizabeth in her progress towards the Church, partly in friendship and sympathy, living with her the events of life—the loss of her mother, fears about death, separation from her husband, joy in their only son, David, who was also Caryll's godson.

30TH SEPTEMBER, 1935

Thank you very much for your letter and for your interest in my article. I am only too glad to discuss the points you raise; it is such a help to clarify one's thoughts by discussing, and still more helpful to learn the thoughts of others about the things one has at heart....

The basic idea of Catholicism *is* the indwelling of the Holy Spirit in man, the Christ-life in the soul, and all that this implies both as regards a man's conduct in his own life and his charity to other men. I am sure that you would be absorbed if you got one or two books on the subject written by good theologians and studied them. I am *not* a theologian and not very well fitted to expound on doctrine, but as I understand it, the doctrine is this: that in every baptized Christian (which means anyone baptized at all, not only those baptized by a Catholic priest, and includes those who have the baptism of desire and of blood)—in the soul of every baptized Christian, Christ lives. He is, as it were, a germ of Christ in them, or a seed of Christ. This seed of Christ grows and flowers in them as they correspond to grace, and the whole object of a Christian is to become "another Christ"—that means, to become Christ: the word "other" or "another" is used just to remind us that though we are capable of being absolutely one with Him, there *is* all the same an otherness about God, otherwise we couldn't adore and serve Him; also though, through grace, we are identified with Him, this is a free gift won for us by the Incarnation of Christ, and we are still men dependent on Him for our very being.

What you say in your letter about seeing the spirit of God in others suggests that your ideal is in perfect harmony with the Catholic ideal of the Christ-life, and, as you say, "at this rate all men ought to be at peace with one another." This peace most certainly *would* exist if all men were, as they could be, words of God, other Christs and visible manifestations of the Holy Spirit abiding in them. But as it is, this is not the case: to start with, Christ has told us that there is a condition which must be fulfilled if He is to dwell in us—namely, that we keep His word. To hear it, to accept it as beautiful and desirable and yet to go on living as if it applied to others in act, to ourselves only as a pious and lovely theme for thought, is useless—we have to keep it, to live by it, to obey it. Here is what He says: "If anyone loveth me, he will keep my word, and my Father will love him and we will come to him, and will make our abode with him." And here again is the other side of the picture in His words: "If anyone abide not in me, he shall be cast forth as a branch, and shall wither, and they shall gather him up, and cast him into the fire, and he burneth."

So it is clear that in some people the seed of Christ withers and even dies, and though He is potentially in them (God still causes their being—otherwise they would cease to be; and because of their baptism they are able to receive the grace of sorrow for sin, and to repent, and if they do, Christ will rise again in them), none the less, so long as they remain in sin (grave sin, of course), Christ is *not* alive in them, and other people cannot see Him or His spirit manifested in them.

Therefore we cannot after all look complacently about us, see Christ in all men and make an end of war. What we can do, however, is strive to make the life of Christ visible in us, to make it a reality in our own souls. This is exactly what I meant in my article "to live by faith." ...

The tragedy of modern England is an almost complete lack of any real education in faith. Ask the average man fresh from a public school what he has learnt there of religion, of the spirit: he will tell you, nothing, or something so vague that it amounts to nothing. The same applies to the average man from the elementary school; and normally the home life of both has done nothing to supply the want. It is impossible for a young person to be totally devoid of religion, for adoration is an instinct of human nature, so most people do work out a religion of their own. They feel the need of something to give coherence and meaning to their lives; in the case of the more generous, they feel the need to give, to serve, to justify themselves, and so, at all events for a time, they try to work it out in their own minds. In some cases they go a long way towards spiritual success and "make their souls" in a way which must surely please God, but in most cases as they grow older they grow more dependent on, and more contented with, material things. Life is full of distraction, anxieties and temptations, and the spiritual sense becomes blunted and finally quiescent—and we get the vast multitude who, whilst normally seeking their own advantage at the expense of anyone who stands in their way, assure us blandly that their religion is "kindness," varied by city dwellers who are able on rare occasions to "worship God on the hilltop," or, for the less keen hikers, "in a garden"—and sadder still, the crowds and crowds who practically cease to think at all and try pathetically to live by "bread alone."

Now, to be educated in faith means to have learnt what God has revealed and to have proved it experimentally, so far as one can, by obeying Him. God is Truth: our minds cannot comprehend the entire truth; our longing for Truth can help us towards goodness, but since we are human and not infinite we can only know truth through faith—through learning what God, who *is* Truth, has revealed, and living by it. This implies not only education of the mind but of the spirit. Actually a person of the meanest intelligence can have an educated spirit, for prayer brings one closer to truth than thought, and the lessons of the spirit are humility, obedience, sacrifice and love. I do not say that I *condemn* anyone for lack of faith. Not at all; faith is a gift, to start with, and secondly, not everyone is altogether responsible even if, having received the gift, it fails in them. We can never assess human responsibility or condemn anyone, but a man without faith is to be pitied, and the vague yearning for "something," plus toying with thought, is not faith; neither is a whole mass of knowledge about literature and the craftsmanship in art. The education which I believe would enable people to appreciate the *beauty* in art (that is, the idea giving a work of art form, in the philosophical sense, the form of it) is the education which teaches man that the soul is more than the body, that eternity is more important than time, that God has absolute sovereignty over man, that to Him we owe absolute obedience, that austerity and mortification, not only of the senses but of the intellect, are essential to salvation, and essential even to genuine happiness on earth. Such education requires only that a man has a good will for its foundation, and *can* be given to everyone. The surest way of getting this education is to desire truth and goodness, for desire fits one to receive what one desires, and the person who does, in spite of the difficulties of a post-Christian England, keep alive this desire, is almost certain to achieve what he seeks—"Ask and you shall receive.…"

The second part of your question, which I've just been answering, is whether you can get people all to apprehend God in the same way. I have only to repeat myself, but to try to be clear I will. There is God, the Supreme Spirit. We can know almost nothing about Him; we can know that He exists by reason; so far as He can be revealed to our finite minds at all, He is revealed by Christ. We can't receive much—picture a child of four asking how to drive a car; you wouldn't attempt to explain the works of it, you'd show him "You press this, you turn that," and so on. What you tell him is true, but it is by no means the truth as *you* know it. So it is with God and us; we can't all arrive at the same conclusion about God by ourselves, because any, or almost any, ideas we can conceive with finite minds about Infinity must be wrong, or at least very far short of Truth—but since Truth, God, is not something composed by us, made up of our ideas, but is absolute and real, we *can* all agree about Him if we accept *His* Revelation of Himself. But if not, then we cannot; not only nations cannot, but two in one family cannot. But you don't say "believe in God in the same way," but "apprehend Him"; well, *that* we all do differently, for apprehending is an inner knowing; it is intimate and personal; it is like putting out your hand in the dark and finding someone else's hand stretched out to you, and somehow knowing that this is the hand of one you love.

We have all our own secret apprehensions of God. The lives of the saints show us in a vivid way how diverse all these ways are, the huge variety of personal inspirations from God to man, the extraordinary way in which God, who is one and simple, comes to flower in the souls of men in unbelievable variety, just like God being the cause of all the innumerable flowers we see in nature, yet single and one and unchanging Cause of them all.

The variety of human experience of God is all *within* Revelation and never opposed to it, so that in Christ men can be one and yet not lose their individuality, freedom of will or personal inspiration.... When we do all accept the Revelation of Christ, I say with certainty that we will have the Kingdom of Heaven on earth. I mean, of course, that this will be so when we not only all believe but live in harmony with our belief, for the failure of some epochs of faith has not been faith but the frailty of the faithful—and I say with certainty that we can be one in faith and in knowledge of truth and can have peace among nations and individuals, if we become as little children and accept the Word. My certainty is the word of God: "And the glory which thou hast given me, I have given to them: that they may be one, as we also are one. I in them and thou in me, that they may be made perfect in one, and the world may know that thou hast sent me, and hast loved them as thou hast also loved me." ...

19TH NOVEMBER, 1937

I heard today of your mother's very sudden death, and I want to tell you how very deeply I feel for you in what I know must be a great sorrow as well as a dreadful shock to you. I won't say what I'm sure will be said to you over and over again—that she was spared a long illness and pain. It's true, but that does not take away from the fact of the greater shock to *you* because you had no warning. I can only pray that Our Lord, who is so truly both Father and Mother to us all, will Himself give you whatever thoughts are most likely to be comforting to you; and while I pray for you in this way, I thank Him too for the fact that you have Louis to look after you, and I am certain he will be to you now what no one else could be.

When this grief is a little more in the past, I am sure you, who have faith, will feel that death doesn't part people but brings them closer, and those who see things from God's side understand us more than even the nearest could on earth. I feel sure that over and over again you will know that your mother's love will be helping and guiding you and darling David, and you will know how true it is "there is no death." …

10TH OCTOBER, 1942

… I haven't been indifferent about answering your letter, but have *not* been able to find the good stretch of time which I felt that it required. Actually it has been in my pocket since I had it, and it has been read and re-read over and over again, and that with the deepest sympathy and joy. Joy, because I feel certain that you *will* be able to resolve your difficulties and to become a Catholic—and that I long for, partly for obvious reasons which need not be stated, and also because it is clearly the happiest and loveliest thing possible for David. And finally Louis! Well, Louis' delight will be beyond everything.…

I think the long time you have been pondering things, good, because I am sure you are too fine, too big and genuine and too capable of real holiness to become a Catholic excepting as the result of your own experience; and your own experience does of course include loving and marrying Louis, being David's mother and so on. Christ said "I am the Way," and I am sure that the search and longing for Him, the things that bring you closer to Him, and even the periods of doubt, mental fatigue and resentment, are all means of union with Him. So that it would be silly and wrong not to realize that every prayer said in any church, every act of love to everyone, every doubt or question honestly entertained, is a means of union with Him; and He includes that meaning in "I am the Way."

20TH NOVEMBER, 1942

… Dear Elizabeth, *don't* hesitate to argue, disagree, say if something is not clear, because I only want you to sift as deeply as you can, and my object is to help you to do so; *not* to "convince" you by poor arguments, but to tell you some facts about the Church which you can turn over in your own mind—because I am perfectly sure that no one really discovers Truth as a living thing excepting through their own experience and in their own way.

First you say you find that you can only get direct spiritual contact with God when you are alone, not in church.

The object that Christ founded the Church for was (and is) to give people direct contact—union—with Him, and the reason for going to church and for receiving the sacraments is to have this union. There is no doubt at all that when you are in church, and when you are alone, and in fact wherever you are and in whatever circumstances, you do always have this union with God, but you become more aware of it when you are alone. This is not surprising: there are fewer distractions alone, and not only fewer exterior but fewer interior ones; and besides that, you are a very individual person, and it is natural that you should prefer solitary prayer and awareness of God. There is no harm in it, none at all, but I am sure that if you did receive the Sacrament you would find that, far from being impoverished by it, your solitude would be enriched and your awareness of God intensified. Every Holy Communion is like (and in fact is) a renewal of the Christ-life in the soul, and when you go out of church after Mass, you go with (to use a silly and inaccurate expression)—you go with *more*, not less, of the presence of God in your soul. The great point is that Christ has chosen to give Himself in a particular way, through a particular means—namely the sacraments: and the sacraments are given in church (normally).

A point about this which I have always found very touching is when, at the Last Supper, Christ was about to give the Blessed Sacrament to the Apostles, He said, "With desire have I desired this hour"— that is to say, "I have longed for this hour." He surely meant these words not *only* for the Apostles, but for everyone who would receive Him in Communion. He longed for this hour in which He would give Himself to us; I don't doubt that He longs equally for the hour when each person receives Communion now.

After He had died and risen again, I should think it more than likely that some among the Apostles were best able to pray alone, like you; that in solitude they could recall all He said and did more easily and were more able to realize His presence better able, too, to realize His presence in themselves. But all the same, one can't imagine that they, who were present at the Last Supper, would ever have deliberately stayed away from Holy Communion.

9TH DECEMBER, 1942

… Your fear of death is the thing which is really easiest to start with and goes straight to other things.…

Death is a punishment for sin. God did not create man to die; He created him to live. He did not condition man to want to die; on the contrary, He gave him fierce instincts to resist and fight death, and made the longing for life so strong that it remains natural to cling to life even in the most wretched circumstances. Death is not something in

God's plan; it is not something (to use a very odd expression) *natural* to God, and the more you retain your likeness to God, so much the more are you likely to dread and hate death and all that relates to it.

There is plenty of evidence that Christ was afraid of His death; read the description of the Agony in the Garden and compare it with His reiterated praise and love of life ("I came that they should have life and have it more abundantly," etc.).

10TH NOVEMBER, 1942

Yes, God *is* life and the cause of life, and death is something contrary to God's will, brought into the world by sin....

We were created in God's image: that means that we were created with a natural love of life, with a tendency towards everything vital and productive and flowering and fruitful, and we were created to love. Love *is* in a sense the procession and renewal of life from generation to generation—

> *From Genesis to genesis*
> *Life has trembled in a kiss.*

Well, then, if the love of life and fear of death prove you to have kept, rather than have lost, something of your likeness to God—what is the attitude of the Church to death? She accepts it as a punishment, and because the punishment comes from the tender hand of a Father, she accepts even with joy; and because she believes in eternal life she realizes that death is something which has to be gone through to come to eternal life (though it certainly would *not* have been the gate to life, had we not sinned); and she aims at teaching her children to face it bravely, and to look beyond it—she tells them that just because it *is* so hard to nature, we really help to redeem the world when we suffer our deaths bravely for God's love. She teaches that death does not separate people, because the soul is never dead, so that although [with] the parting, the millions of tiny physical details of bodily love and closeness have gone, and the agony of *that* remains, the person has not gone and remains alive and close to the living.

She teaches that we can help the dead by praying for those in Purgatory, and that they can and do pray for us. She has, of course, great reverence for dead bodies, because they have been the temples of the Holy Spirit; more, because Christ dwelt in them and was homely there; they were His home (that is to say, *body* and *soul united*, and they *are* one for all practical purposes in this world).

You see, fear of death is right.…

14TH DECEMBER, 1942

… The fear of death, as I said yesterday, is natural and right, but the Church *does* teach us gradually to overcome this fear—not always by removing it, but by giving us the strength to suffer it, so that, after some time of receiving the sacraments and living with the Faith, a change takes place.…

The average Catholic child grows up fairly familiar with the idea of death, and provided he does understand the spiritual side of it—and he usually does—he is never likely to be swamped by the fear of it.

But—and this comes straight up to the Blessed Sacrament—no one can hope to get the balance that makes fear of death, or any other fear, tolerable if they rely on themselves, or intellectual ideas, or their own efforts of will. They can only hope through one thing—namely, the actual fact of the presence of Christ in them.

1ST APRIL, 1944

… I am determined that after what human beings have suffered in this war, I personally just could not rest unless I re-order my life so that it is as worth while as it *can* be in future. What I mean is that it is my absolute belief that Christianity alone can do any good in the world now; and when I say "do any good," I do not mean—produce economic reform, or better drains, or a fuller medical service, or brighter trade unions. I'm not meaning to belittle such reforms, etc., but whereas they have come to mean everything to a lot of thinking people, I believe that they would be the inevitable result of Christianity; but aiming at them without a very definite Christianity *first* is futile. What I do mean by Christianity is:

(a) First of all what Christ taught. We *can't* solve half the problems asking for solutions, but He knows all the answers; and in any case a Christian state or world, built on one or two things He taught, plus a vague desire for a "better world," is nonsense.

Secondly (or "b"!): by Christianity I mean a faith which will give some coherent answer to the difficulties about suffering, the suffering of innocence in particular: that will give people comfort in suffering (in the true sense of the word "comfort," i.e. "to make strong"): that will guarantee and somehow keep fast the ideal of love, and will keep human love and [love of] the world as its first value, and which will increase *life*, spiritual and physical, at all times, in all circumstances.

It would take too long to enlarge on what a blessing to mankind other things in our Faith are, such as *sorrow* for sin, for instance. But what I want to explain is that I think myself that the most constructive thing one *can* do in this world is to make the Christian Faith *known* to English people. I have been absolutely astonished during this war to find how *very few* of the people who talk about a better world based on Christianity have even a rough idea of what Christ taught—other than a very vague idea that it is "love"; and I have met more than one who thinks this "love" means the same thing as a slap and tickle on Hampstead Heath!

When I think of Europe and Greece, of all those little kids hungry, of little Greek children who have learnt to know when they are going to die and lay themselves down in the street and tidy their own rags to do it—and the men who have died, and of the hundreds—millions, in fact—of little families like your own that have had to be parted during the sweetest years of life; of millions of fathers like Louis who have had to miss so much of their little sons' babyhood—it makes me mad, and it makes it impossible for me to consider doing anything but my *very best* after the war....

III

To Baroness Bosch van Drakestein

As war drew near, Caryll had begun her work at the First Aid Post. She was at the same time writing most of the Children's Messenger, *the editor of which was a sick man, and also many articles for the* Grail Magazine. *She had formed a warm friendship with Yvonne Bosch van Drakestein, who had brought the Grail to England in 1932. These letters illuminate the time and place—London during the Second World War— which were to open for Caryll a wide apostolate and develop her powers to carry it out.*

7 MILBORNE GROVE
26TH AUGUST, 1939

… It struck me last night that many people are increasing their fear by thinking in crowds, i.e. they think of hundreds and thousands suffering, etc., whilst the fact is, God is thinking of each one of us separately; and when—say—a hundred or a million are suffering, it is God who has each *one* separately in His own hands and is Himself measuring what each *one* can take, and to each one He is giving His illimitable love. This thought, though obvious, consoles me a lot.…

Still, there is hope of peace, and I hope most eagerly, and am off now to say a prayer to the martyr [John Southworth] in the Cathedral.

26TH AUGUST, 1939

It was *lovely* to hear your voice tonight; I did really feel about at the end of my tether—very zeroish!—the house so dark and empty, and outside it the continual sound of aeroplanes and heavy traffic—and this sort of quiet agony inside oneself....

Now I do feel we've just got to shut our eyes and dive into this sea of Christ—dive with the trust of people who can't swim and yet go straight into the dark water.

We may be spared still, and one understands so well now our dear Lord's prayer in Gethsemene, His fear, and His courage. But whatever happens in the future, it seems to me that in this which we are *now* experiencing, He is saying, "Fear not, it is I." I can't explain, but several times today, when I felt I could really cave in, suddenly, right in the midst of *myself*, His voice seemed to say that, "Fear not, it is I," and I felt vaguely that somehow or other our *becoming* Christ—the consummation of our love for Him—has to take this form of knowing something of His Passion, so that even the feeling of fear, and the awful moments when one just wants to cry and cry like a child, need not shame us, because they are all part of Christ's own experience in us.

I can't make my meaning clear, but I shall try to hang on to the thought all the time that, in a mysterious way, everything that happens to us is not only His will, but Himself.

31ST AUGUST, 1939

... Tonight hope of peace is slender indeed; it is true that, if God wills, it may yet be, but humanly one hopes but little now.

Caryll Houselander

For my part, I do realize more and more that "all is well" either way, peace or war, for the "peace of God" which just now we taste is so utterly different from any of the substitutes for it which in the past we have tried to be content with.

The thing that hurt me most in this whole business was the idea that the human race *could* be dragged into a thing of such violence, so utterly against the principles of the Sermon on the Mount—creating circumstances, it seemed, in which the simple beauty of life preached by Christ Our Lord were obliterated.

But now that great anguish has left me. It came to me like a blinding flash of light that Christ did not resist evil, that He allowed *Himself* to be violently done to death, that when He gave *Himself* to be crucified, He knew that the exquisite delicacy and loveliness of the merest detail of Christian life would survive the Passion, that indeed, far from being destroyed by it, it depended on it.

And so it is now: that which is holy, tender and beautiful will not be swept away or destroyed by war; on the contrary, we can still say, "Ought not Christ to suffer these things and so enter into His glory?"

Never has my own heart so proved to me that the direct "contemplation" of Christ in men, in the world—done not only through our minds, but through our bodies also—is the way to Him, the way to heaven on earth: and now I see how, without more than a necessary amount of egoism, we can contemplate Him in our own life and come closer to Him through it. This last means a more intense living and perhaps a more intense dying.

I am confident now that the poetry, the beauty of life, which is nothing else but our divine Lord living in human souls, will go on, and that our lives, though they seem to leave no visible trace, will not have been in vain.

Now it seems so different to face war if it comes—not so much a bracing of self to face horror (that, it *has* been), but now, more as if one were just a child, unable any longer to resist the love of a mother, and so opening one's hand for the nails gently, just—as it were—becoming still, unresisting.

"Thy will be done" is no longer a mere word of resignation, but more like a marriage vow—but more, far more than that: a becoming *one* with Him, which casts out fear, fear for self, and fear for humanity....

The supreme comfort for me is that the war which is threatened will not *disturb* our contemplation of Christ, but will complete it.

As I write this to you, it seems to me that one sound, or one pulse, rather, fills the world—the beating of the heart of Christ, and so full of love it is that one wishes only to put one's own heart into it, to live and die in His Passion with Him....

I think that, whether there is a war or whether there is not, it would be a very good idea to have the next Grail Magazine on the Lord's Prayer (the Our Father).

Briefly my reasons: it is simple and vital, it contains everything we should pray, it is illimitably deep, profoundly simple, it answers both all our needs in war and our needs and direction to build up peace if we are again given the chance. It contains our whole attitude to others, too. It can be done in not too heavy, yet not at all flippant, a way.

That is good; if the war comes, we will have to repeat a prayer by heart, almost automatically: the more meaning it has for us, the more help it will be. If it is peace, we will be tired, we will want *something*, but something to rest in and yet grow strong in....

2ND SEPTEMBER, 1939

... I have had a busy day (that warning we heard, by the by, was simply that a 'plane was seen over the Channel which could not immediately be identified, so they thought it best to warn us). I am sorry to say that sooner or later we are bound to be bombed: it may be tonight, or may not be for months, and of course we *may* keep them off—but we have to expect it and be ready.

My dear, we must pray for one another. For my part, I am a great coward, and I know I am going to be *more* and *more* afraid. But with our trust in God—with our hands in His—all will be well: "Under us are the eternal arms." ...

When the first days of this agony are over, it is going to lead on from suffering to suffering in every way—fear, loss, death—one can't bear to think of it. Our work is to keep alive a deep, constant awareness of the living *love* of God; to be, as never before, contemplatives of Christ in ourselves and in one another; to keep His Passion before us and to keep our faith in His love, never allowing the despair and pessimism which must sweep many hearts to shake ours.

The *way of* teaching, telling, helping people to believe will have to be different. It is now forbidden to assemble big crowds of people together (owing to added danger in case of raids).... From the Grail point of view, it seems to me good. It will force what *I*, at all events, have desired for a long time—i.e. the intensifying of real life in the world—and it will kill anything in the way of big-scale organizing. In other words, it has to be the kingdom *within* or nothing! The members must be engaged in national service, which is in itself service of humanity, and demands a heavy toll on each, and we ought to help them to carry into every place they go and all they do the one idea of the deep, abiding love of Christ Our Lord, which, far from being destroyed now, breaks out into flower even in *our* weak frightened hearts....

(UNDATED)

When I came in last night, Iris called me to her bedside and said, "Go quickly and draw our chestnut buds—their little hands are folded in prayer, and tomorrow they will spread them out and say, 'Dominus vobiscum'!" So I went down to the sitting-room where we have the buds, and drew them, and sure enough they are tiny hands with little thin wrists, praying! Yesterday they had woolly vests on like babies, and by tonight I think their hands will be open. It is so *lovely* to think that all over England they are opening these small green hands and crying "Dominus vobiscum" to the world!

That is just what I want to say to you, because that is our "message": "The Lord be with you and with your spirit."

I am happy that you feel strongly for this Christing of the world. It seems to me that, just as the Nazi menace is, materially, sweeping through Europe and driving people out of their kingdoms, their homes, a great wave of spiritual Naziness (very like *nastiness*) is sweeping through England and in a yet more deadly fashion driving people out of the inward kingdom of their souls—out of their home, Christ. For certainly…we can be sure that Christ wants to make His *home* in our hearts: "If any man come to me, I will in no wise send him away": "And we will come to him and make our abode in him."

This "abode" means more than a residence: it means "where I abide, where I *live* always, where I am at home, at peace, where I may rest and sleep, where I can be wholly and simply myself, where, too, I can reveal my secret, shed my tears, ease my sorrows."

This, then, is surely the desire of our sweet Lord's own heart, that He shall be at *home* in us—that we shall receive His tears and His sorrows in our own hearts secretly, that we shall not let the world with its unrest disturb that stillness where He may rest and be at peace; that in us, when He wills, He shall sleep.

To become aware of Him like this makes us realise that *everything else but Christ is passing*, but is a necessary passing thing which is part of His Passion and life in this passing world. For so long as we let fear of war, loathing of Catholic Action, etc., etc., afflict us, we cannot be in peace, we cannot be silent, empty to receive Him into His home. But also, for so long as we believe that our activities, our vocations, are going to have an effect which Christ's own life on earth did *not* have—so long as we "organize" for a *visible* kingdom—we shall not be at peace.

"Perfect love casts out fear." We have to begin to love Him in so intimate a way that even a war, though it could shatter our nerves, shall not touch our peace: for surely, if *everything* that happens to us means one thing only—Christ with us, Emmanuel—what does it matter how we die or even how we live? We begin now to be in heaven, and heaven is for eternity.

F.A. 1
(as from Milborne Grove)
Wednesday

… All that I can see clear is that the time now has come when everybody is offered a chance of living the Christ-life and contemplating Him *directly*, and how well this is done will not depend on their understanding of it, but on their *doing* of it.

I am sure just as many non-Catholics as Catholics are learning the Christ-life this day, almost perfectly.

It seems to me that what matters is to create in this world a force of *love* strong enough to combat that of hate—and more particularly of fear. If we are ever to come back to the lovely morning of Christianity, we must not do it by waiting for the war to end; it has to be done now, through love. If each individual can put into her personal life an unstinted, absolute love, then already out of these dark days Christ will be reborn.

I do so agree with you that the official hate propaganda is one of the very greatest tragedies of war, and there ought to be a continual quiet resistance of it, where met. I do not think, however, that one will prevail much on those who feel such a hate by trying to make them think kindly of Hitler: *but* if, day after day, love grows in the individual heart, it will both keep alive that heart and wipe out all elements of hate. There is not room for love and hate in one heart.

I feel strongly that, so far as the "written word" is concerned, you should issue merely the simple statements of facts: how this war is Christ's Passion—how Christ's Passion redeems—how we are all "other Christs," and so are now invited to enter His Passion. And so on—just simple facts. And I think it wise to let each in her own way, and in the degree in which God gives her grace, apply this to her own life.

To give orders, or even too definite advice—I should hesitate. As things are, we now are suddenly plunged into a most gruelling discipline which far exceeds in its severity any ever known in school or religious order.

Everything we want to do now, we have to give up, for more or less all the time, and our dearest friends are now separated from us and are in the shadow of death. We have to be cheerful and brave, and we realize that our individual sorrow is the common sorrow of all the world. There is no room for *more* orders, advice, or self-discipline.

No, on the contrary, what is needed is a deeper knowledge of Christ and all that can *soften* and make more lovely this life.

With all the extraordinary means which we are compelled to take to preserve our bodies, we have to remember that to preserve the beauty, gentleness and balance of the *human mind* will need far more defences—and these are almost neglected. Thus, more even than before we ought to learn to become more deeply aware of beauty around us, when it *is* around us, and to appreciate the poetry and loveliness of the mind.

It seems to me that at Eastcote you should offer peace, a refuge, where in the presence of the Blessed Sacrament people can get right away from war, can sleep, can see flowers and untroubled skies, and can so far as possible build up their nerves for what is to be suffered.

I would certainly have there, before others, those who have *not* got a country home or refuge—the poorer ones.

I do not think that *anything* need be, or should be, added to this work. A house of peace, where you can keep and give Christ and knowledge of Christ as the stronghold of the mind, defending the inward kingdom of love.

In all our defences, this one defence does not exist, and on it depends whether this great force of natural courage, generosity and kindness will flame into such a fire of reparation and love that God, for Christ's dear sake, will accept our offering and forgive our poor world and give us peace. As to the future, after the war, that also depends on one thing alone—whether we *start* that longed-for peace with the spirit of primitive, poor Christianity, or not....

7 Milborne Grove
17th September, 1939

... Gradually we are adjusting ourselves to what I can only call a new and different world. It is amazing how much has happened inwardly to nearly everyone, and in a few days. One thing which is in some ways frightening is the fact that only very few people seem to have "come over" with one. I mean that, of the vast number of people one knows, one realizes that in this "other world" there are hardly any of them with whom one has or will have any real personal contact. Real contact, real communion with anyone now seems to depend on whether or not both realize the Passion of Christ in the same way, and whether there is a strong love to make this realization understood without much talk about it.

I have had some very, very bad moments, with a sheer physical desire to weep—but never, so far, *any* desire to get out of any of it or of what may come. At last it seems to me I have been allowed to taste the rim of the cup of Christ's Passion—only the rim, it is true, but even that goes very deep. Just the fact of having to go so *completely* against my own will in *everything* at the F.A. Post seems to give me a sense of abnegation which somehow seems to contain the very essence of love... I go to it as to a lovers' meeting.... Often I have drawn the crucifix, and now I know I shall draw it on myself.

You know how often I've written or said that one wants to say to Our Lord, "If I can't ease your suffering, anyhow let me be there, let me be with you." I think it's that—all these years His Passion going on, and though I've wrestled against my own indulgences I've put up such a poor show: and now we actually *are* allowed to be with Him, to feel His Passion in ourselves and to be constrained to give up at once all those things we couldn't before.

Of course, so far I'm miles away from entering His Passion as I would like to—because, to tell the truth, the love I have for Him seems as much to be possessing and dominating me as the suffering round us, and on my days at home—half my life still—I have been particularly indulgent to myself. I have not yet got adjusted well enough to do my work, and I have been hard put to keep patient with all the people who come, and who so much need to be loved back to peace. I shall have to pray a lot before the little spark of my own life can truly be called reparation—and I am sure that reparation, whatever form it takes, is the supreme war work in this war.

It makes it hard for me that most people who come, come to *get* peace from me, not to give it. Human contacts are so precious now, and I do so want strong people. I want also to receive the comfort of fellow creatures....

I have two ideas which I'd like to carry out. One I have mentioned here and there and several persons are eager to cooperate, but I do not know if they have the financial means.

One is to make some nice "holy cards," and on the back to print some words of Our Lord about peace and love, or any other words likely to show that Christians desire peace and love and do not foster hatred: and to have these words printed in English, French, German, Polish and Russian. These holy cards I intend to be circulated among the troops; they could be given to men going to the front and to nurses and so on, and I hope they might come into the hands of the enemy, through prisoners, etc. This is a small thing, but it would be a word of love among Christians—and the war of wars now is between love and every other force in the world....

The other thing I'd like would be to take some hoardings, or anywhere suitable, and put up some religious posters—only the simplest things, no abstract ideas, only things that people, all people, *can* see and understand. For example, Our Lady with her Child, and a prayer to our Mother to look after all her children: the Holy Child, and a prayer for the spirit of childhood to come back to us: and again, the crucifix. Also, if it were possible, some of the crucifixes inside air raid shelters—though I daresay the Government would not allow the latter.

We could do so much in a silent way, without any self-advertisement or beastly "propaganda" spirit, to bring just the simple, comforting things of faith before people's eyes. And God knows there is need. Preaching is *more* hateful than ever, but who could not be glad to be reminded, silently, by a picture, that we have a mother, that she can and will care for all mothers' sons? ...

1ST OCTOBER, 1939

... You know I am a very insufficient, frightened, helpless creature: I have no genius, only a little talent, and my only idea is to contemplate Christ in His life in people, for so long as I live among people on earth, and to do it with my whole being—hands, head, heart, etc.: not only with the mind.

It is very simple. Of the next life I have no imagination; it is something that I never think of. Here on earth Christ is almost visible, and because He is in us and with us, I agree with St. Catherine that "all the way to heaven *is* heaven."

But I must say that, though my ideas were simple before the war, they are more simple still now. If I survive it, I am sure that I shall never again return to the compromise that pre-war life was: I have seen and heard and learnt too much already from the war.

I used to smart, to rage, at the worldliness of so-called Christianity, and to come close on despair. Now I see that such so-called Christianity existed, and does, even now; but it isn't the real thing. The real thing, however, exists; it is in the hearts of simple people, and it depends, not upon what school one grew up in, or what creed one believes in, but on one's capacity for love and for humility.

I am sure, as never before, that the Russian idea of Christ, humble, suffering and crowned with thorns, is the only true one; that it is impossible to be a Christ unless the humility and poverty of Christ is taken literally, and all that tends towards power, grandeur, success and so on is avoided and despised.

So simple is the way, that in this fact alone there is joy; it is wonderful, too, to see how this flowering of Christ continues in the human heart and is indeed a seed sown by the Spirit wherever He wills to sow it....

So changed is the world by Germany having simply handed over the power of Europe to Stalin, that there will no longer be the possibility of *tepid* Christianity; but how it will end no one can guess.…

IV

To a Correspondent Who Had Sent Her a Cry for Help

I must say I am glad, selfishly, that I could not come to see you, because I could not have brought myself to give you what I presume would have been the "right" advice: I should have been weak, I should have felt too deep a sympathy with you and too much compassion for your husband.

Your problem was an abnormally and terribly hard one and only sanctity could really drink the cup offered to you; but God knows our hearts and the strength of the things that assail us and the meaning of all that is incomprehensible to us. I am sure that His mercy is surrounding you.

Have you absolutely assured yourself of the validity of your husband's first marriage? If not, do look into it. Also, I think it would be a real help to you to acquaint yourself with Fr. R.H.J. Steuart, S.J. (Farm Street). He would, I am sure, have a deep sympathy and would be a help to you and your husband.

I can only say this; you have wrestled for a long time with an agonizing problem; you have in the course of that struggle shown your true love of God by terrible sacrifices done for Him; your husband too *tried* to do an almost superhuman thing out of love for *your* love of God; so that however sad you may feel now (in one way), you can assure yourself that those moments in which the love of God in you rose to such heroism are always present to God: He will always see you in those great moments of love for Him, and He will never allow someone who has given Him those moments of love to be lost. I only beg of you one thing—namely, do not cease ever to trust in God's love and mercy for you. I am afraid you will not be happy, fundamentally, and I am afraid that, starved of the sacraments as you will be, you may come upon times when you will be tempted to let the Kingdom of God slip away from you; you may even be tempted to despair one day. Well, when and if that happens, do remember that with God there is no past and future, and your moments of utter *love for Him* are always present to Him, and He will never let you perish.

No, you don't seem "dreadfully weak" to me; I only wonder how you managed ever to be so dreadfully strong—I could not have done what you did, for a week!

You are so right to go to Mass and pray, and so brave in the way you face facts and do not try to twist things, in spite of such very awful provocation. I am sure you will be given grace in abundance and the whole thing will come right.

I am bound to say that I think few things more cruel for a child than to see her parents separated; I know by experience, for mine separated when I was nine, so I am glad your little girl is spared. But I shall pray hard and often that God will help you and either remove the stumbling-block or make you saints, so that you can live together, but in abstinence. But of course I know that that is nearly impossible.

The tragedy is that sexual love is such a right and holy thing in itself, which makes it harder than ever to deny it in a case like yours.

I'm afraid this is a poor letter. I wish I had the power to counsel and comfort you well, but I can only pray for you, and that I most surely will do, and do you also pray for me—and please, if it is ever *any* help to you to write to me, do so. I've destroyed your letter.

V

To Archie Campbell-Murdoch (1941–1949)

*The earlier of these letters were to help both
Archie Campbell-Murdoch and his wife Sheila
to overcome their problems in approaching the Church.
A close friendship grew up between them and Caryll,
Iris Wyndham, with whom Caryll lived for so many years,
and her other convert friend, Henry Tayler. Caryll
found them eager to join with her in the various
schemes of apostolate which her fertile brain devised.
The first of these letters shows her already beset
by the troubled people of all kinds begging her help
who became as time went on
a major problem in Caryll's life.*

26TH NOVEMBER, 1941

I do not know how to thank you and Sheila enough for your wonderful kindness in offering me sanctuary in your flat....

I hope to solve the problem [of getting any writing done] by wresting one free day now, as, if I get into the Censorship, no one will know when that day is. It seems to me that somehow or other one *ought* to be strong-minded enough to work in one's home unassailed, but it is a great problem. Actually, even if one can escape in body, one's mind remains guilt-obsessed, accusing and restless, haunted by tottering old ladies, subversive and oversensitive youths, frustrated geniuses, spineless adolescents, dying priests, doubting Anglican clergymen, repressed Catholic nuns, neurasthenic nurses, and the uncountable multitude of weeping free-lance virgins. No four walls, alas, can remove their loneliness and restlessness and the monotony of their lives from the stricken conscience. Yet in truth, I think it likely that one does them more harm than good by sympathy, and that the right thing to do is to steel the heart.

I truly believe that the best way to benefit humanity is to make faces in the bus—slightly mad faces, or puttings out of the tongue suddenly at the person opposite. Think of the thrill *that* gives to countless uneventful lives to whom nothing ever happens. They can tell everyone for weeks that they saw a mad woman on the bus, and they can exaggerate this to almost any extent. This form of charity can be practiced on the way to work.

The house at Milborne Grove had been damaged in the Blitz and now stood empty, but Caryll often wrote in good weather in her shed in the tiny but lovely garden. She heads this letter:

AS FROM NELL GWYNN HOUSE
(REALLY AT MILBORNE GROVE)

Thank you very much for your letter. I'm awfully glad you wrote it, and hope you will go on (I mean go on writing letters about the things that puzzle you), and I will always answer as far as I am capable....

First, then, about the paradoxes in the Gospels. I'll take the last bit of your question first: "How is one to understand the Gospels?" I think the answer is that we have to interpret them *within* the limit which the Church allows and to accept her decision when things seem to baffle us;

but in saying this (which sounds arrogant at first) I keep in mind that the Church, in claiming authority to have the last word about interpreting the Gospels, allows a far bigger scope of interpretation than the average mind is capable of grasping at all....

Therefore, all round what I'll now say, put a big ring of light, which is the Church's final authority—and by the by it is acknowledging this authority which sends us to beg the imprimatur for books about religion.

First, in general: there is Christ's injunction to "take up the cross daily" as the condition of following Him: and, opposite that, the light burden.

These seem to me to be reconciled by many other sayings, one of them being, "Peace I leave with you; my peace I give unto you: not as the world giveth, do I give unto you." In other words, the condition for *intimacy* with Christ is to open one's arms wide to suffering, but when we realize this suffering as *His* suffering, it does not crush us, but on the contrary we discover that love makes it light.

A way to grasp what I mean is to compare it to an earthly love. Take the case of a girl who loves a man who is poor and has been disgraced, and the condition for being with him is sharing in his sufferings. It will certainly mean suffering to accept this, but her only way to happiness lies in accepting it, and once the surrender is made she will discover that the presence of the person she loves, her unity with him, and the very fact of her sharing his suffering, make it a light burden indeed, and the bondage is indeed "easy"!

Christ in heaven is happy, of course, but in man on earth He is identified by His own will with human suffering; and the more we willingly identify ourselves with what is broken and wounded and suffering, the more unity with Him do we have.

Well, that's one way of reconciling those opposite sayings; but there is another point of view.

Christ on earth, what we call the Mystical Body, means one great *living* in all spiritual life. The life of the soul *is* the presence of the Holy Ghost, and the Holy Ghost forms Christ in each of us; but, as Christ is not divided, and, so to speak, cut up to fit into each of us, or each of our lives, the opposite happens—namely, we, who all have the same life, are made into *one* person in Him ("person" used here is all wrong, but will probably convey my meaning!). Now…in Christ everyone exists, *all* experience is known; He has the qualities of the heroes and of helpless children; but we, each of us alone, are finite, very limited. Though Christ in us is *our* whole life, no one of us can lead *His* whole life with all its aspects. For example, we can't be at one and the same time a child, a servant, a king, a poet, and so on: we can't have in us, in its completeness, the character of more than one sort of person. So we actually do live just one tiny detail of His life but, taking us all together united in Him, we make up the Christ on earth, the Mystical Body. Consequently, different passages from the Gospels legitimately appeal to different souls in varying degrees of strength, according to which part they fulfil.

But of course, apart from that, each one *can* hear and respond to all, and those who carry the cross may indeed desire to turn to Him for rest.…

… It does seem to me that in the world we live in, there can be no escape into comfortable piety; that living the Christ-life means, if it is sincere, entering into the work and suffering of the world (into the joy too, in the spirit of Eric Gill). You see, there has been, and still is, though this is nearly incredible, a tendency among religious people to interpret Our Lord's words to mean that it does not matter how soft and selfish the life, so long as you are devout, attend church, etc. Also there has been, and is, too much belief in the Church as a respectable and highly efficient worldly organization, and too little in it as a mysterious unity of saint and sinner, beggar and king.…

P.S. There is a fine and simple book by R.H. Benson called *Paradoxes of Catholicism*. I think it takes *all* the ones in the Gospels.

3RD MARCH, 1942

… (1) About your heart and head. How good that is: naturally your type of mind, united to a generous and gloriously responsive heart, makes the process of being convinced, or of seeking truth, not only a long one but a painful one too: at the same time it makes much more of the journey that is literally wonderful. I mean that you discover so many things on the way, things both of beauty and terror, and when you do come into the harbour you will get the same feeling of sheer magic that one does when one makes one's *first* journey abroad—followed by another amazing discovery—namely, that the haven lands you on a far longer and yet more adventurous journey, and that actually, though you did not know it, you have come in the good old ship of Peter, with quite a lot of good old ecclesiastical barnacles sticking to her bottom (how vulgar that sounds!) and her lovely crimson sails filled with the breath of the Holy Spirit.

You see, she is the only ship that *can* get through the black waters we are sailing, and, thank God, you are in a true sense on her now....

Another point: don't imagine, as some people do, that all your questioning and seeking is a sort of *prologue* to spiritual experience. Of course it is a great spiritual experience in itself, and it is at present your way of union with Christ, who said, "I am the *way*," not simply, "At the end of the way, you find me." Also He said, "I am the Truth" and "Seek and you shall find": so you can be sure that in seeking for truth you are in fact finding Him all the time; and I think that you are getting to know Him with the intimacy that a blind man learns to know a beloved but unseen face, through touching [it] in the darkness—probably a more sensitive awareness than ordinary sight.

But there is a bigger reason to take heart—namely, that your seeking has a purpose for others. Fighting every inch of the way, you are solving many difficulties for others, working it out for them, as Newman did—there was a great intellect for you!—splitting hairs for years. One wonders *why*, until one realizes the hundreds of people who, having the difficulties he had, but not having his courage and character to go on and on fighting them and solving them, have been able to use his experience instead.

St. Catherine of Siena (my favourite saint, by the by, and I think the most enchanting woman that ever lived) said, "All the way to heaven is heaven." I think it is as true to say, "All the way to truth is truth" and "All the way to Christ is Christ." …

14TH APRIL, 1942

Thanks awfully for your letter. I am glad you ask these things, and I am never anything but eager to reply; only I think that in this case Fr. Martindale can do so better, so I've sent you his little book, *Words of Life*—the one I promised. If you turn to p. 32, and read 32, 33 and 34 and 35, you will find, I think, the answer to your problem (a perfectly logical problem, particularly if you have not a full grasp of the doctrine yet). You mentioned once before the same difficulty, and quoted that utterly lovely passage, "Sacrifice and oblation thou wouldst not."

I think this means, *not* the old idea of the slain lamb or kid or whatever it might be, or the burnt offering; not the merely material thing which is only man's gift, anyway, and unworthy of God, though for a time He accepted it: *but* instead the alive and eternal man, the *whole* man, spiritual *and* physical, God and man, Christ: and indeed the end of the same quotation bears out this interpretation. It is: "But a body thou hast fitted to me; then said I, Behold I come. In the head of the book it is written of me that I should do thy will, O God." … It is true, as you say, that the writing (of the Gospels) is the proof of the occasion *now*, and the fact that it *has* been preserved saves us from the additions and subtractions from the truth which would have occurred, had we not the Gospels to check up by. It is, as you doubtless know, the teaching of the Church that the writings in question are inspired; so one must believe—if one believes that—that at the moment when it was to become necessary to have some kind of touchstone for Christian belief, the Holy Ghost, who inspired them, also inspired those who selected them from the mass of other writing which claimed to be true too. There is no reason to think that this same Holy Ghost should later on betray the body that did in fact find and treasure these records and, having in the first place entrusted them to her, now take them from her and hand over the trusteeship to another body—and to a body that interprets them to mean, on most vital points, precisely the opposite to what the original trustees taught, and which was accepted as the true interpretation from the start. Now, it seems to me that God (and of course the Holy Ghost is God) could not be fickle or undecided, or change His mind about what was the truth! But if we admit that the Catholic Church first had and taught the Gospels, that she was guided in selecting the four out of the others, guided in declaring them true, then such an admission is in itself a denial of the validity of the Protestant claim—for to admit it would be the same as saying that after some hundreds of years the Holy Ghost had been mistaken concerning the basic things of faith, and so inspired a new set of men to repudiate all that He had given the first set of inspirees to accept! ...

It is very disagreeable for you to have to have these tiresome interviews, but perhaps they will lead to the recalling of the poor lapsed Catholic. No people on earth so need pity and prayers as lapsed Catholics. I know this, for once, for a short time, I was one—at least, not exactly *lapsed*, but dislocated. I believed in the sacraments, but I could not at the time reconcile the idea of the Church with the hard-heartedness I had met with among many Catholics—a long story, and not interesting. But at the root of the lapse (mine also) there is *nearly always* one of two things—or both of them: pride and sex. Sex, in itself beautiful and utterly holy, so often the stumbling-block, because of our appalling civilization.

Lapsed Catholics are often despised by Catholics. It is very wrong: they ought to be loved and regarded as wounded, and I believe that did they meet with more sympathy and love, they would always come back, even if it were only because, as you so truly say, the Church is home; and to be a lapsed Catholic is, no matter how much bravado is used to hide it, to be endlessly homesick.

We must pray for your mental combatants, and if I were you I would tell them with as much gentleness as possible that whilst you are grateful for their wish to save you, even if it be rather to please your mother than to give glory to God, your salvation is in fact something between yourself and God, and you are not answerable to *anyone* else.

You could recall for your comfort how often people tried to "catch out" Our Lord by posing questions to Him, and though His kindness was absolute He never wasted time in answering this type of question, but silenced them with some question of His own. Sincere questioners who asked in humility got different treatment! …

As from Nell Gwynn House
(really office lunch hour)
11th September, 1942

I can't tell you how I rejoiced in your news, and how deeply grateful I feel that I may come.

When I was a little girl I used to think that I would have liked to be the sheepdog of the Bethlehem shepherds, in order to have got into the stable for the birth of Christ; and since that, I've often thought how much I would have liked to be an insect on a flower or weed near Christ's tomb, in order that I might have seen Him newly risen from the dead.

Very well, you allow me to come and be there when once again He is born into the world, and once again rises from the death we have made life to be. When Christ is renewed in one soul, He is born again and risen again in the whole world; and, knowing this miracle, this re-flowering of a Spring that is eternal, then we can be reassured of the truth that, in spite of all we see, there is resurrection everywhere, and that Love *has* overcome the world.

Now about the actual day and time. Of course I can suit myself to you. I can get a special day if I ask in time—but of course it's a bit late to know what is your best time, as we have to apply for our day on Sunday: you may not have time to let me know before then. I do think the evening a nice time to be received anyway, because if you make your First Communion the next day, you can spend the night in great peace and come to your First Communion without distractions.…

Now you say what day: if it's the evening, all the better: and in any case we will arrange about a little supper that day, not a *party*, just a supper such as the one at Emmaus, a *real* feast....

How about Sheila—is she going to be received before or after or at the same time, and shall you be able to face each other across the table?! Of course you will.

I am worried over the present. I want to give you a crucifix carved by me, but can't possibly hope to have it ready, but I'm sure you won't mind having it a little later on. I think I'll do Our Lady and the Infant Christ for Sheila....

Now, if there is thankfulness going, believe me I thank God for His grace in you and Sheila, and I thank you for having shown me that miracle of Christ in you, and for having been so hungry for Divine Truth that you were able to bear patiently with the spates of talk from me and to pick out the *crumbs* of the bread of life that were there. I am sure we can both live closer to God (a silly expression, but you know what I mean) through the happy, human joy of knowing each other.

I do rejoice with you—and the cold plunge won't really be as bad as you think!

> *The heading of the next letter is corrected from the number of Iris Wyndham's flat into "The Kitchmorgue." This was what Caryll called the very small, dark flat which yet it was a joy to have secured. Here she could, if she chose, work all night—and even the closest friendship gains from periods of solitude.*

12TH NOVEMBER, 1942

How lovely—I will come to the 10.30 Mass, and I hope David[†] will. It will be a really heavenly occasion. When I heard that the church bells

---

[†] Her name for Henry Tayler.

are to ring in London, I literally laughed for joy, for it will seem to us that they are carolling the descent of the Spirit for you!

I have to be at the Censorship at 1 o'clock, so daresay we will get time to feast fittingly, and it is the culmination of so much, and the beginning of so much—perhaps also "the end of the beginning"! ...

3RD JANUARY, 1943
LUNCH HOUR: WORK

Ever since Christmas I have been wanting to write to you, and yet more since I had your lovely letter about the crib—your angel must have guided your hand when you wrote it. You know I had some very bitter trouble over Christmas—I won't bore you with details, but it was as heavy on me as anything could be, and I felt almost as near despairing as I could do. I do not mean despairing of God's mercy, but of my work ever doing anything but go awry and give pain; if you knew all the facts you would know why I felt like that. But when I saw you getting the lights for your little crib, and being, in a real, lovely sense "the father" in your little family, it somehow gathered every spark of what capacity for joy I had left into a point—a point of light, the little light by your crib. And I then had a deep peace in spite of everything, and saw visibly how nothing matters so long as Christ is born again in the souls of men.

It wasn't the crib, but the idea in the crib and the response to it in you that was lovely; and one did really *know* that your goodness and kindness and Sheila's was stronger than all the hard things that can happen.

So, for me too, a Christmas which might have been among the saddest has been one which I shall remember always as particularly lovely—in fact, I feel sure that in time what I shall remember will be only the lovely things. I believe that you feel the same exactly about the inward side of Christmas as I do; and how it does increase joy to share it! It is odd how love between friends does increase joy and lessen grief—surely another application of "If two or three are together in my name I will be with them" (misquoted, but right sense!). I think you and I and Sheila and Iris and David have between us every ingredient of a really happy Christmas. I hope next year we will again be together and David with us, and I don't forget Brigid[†]: she is the essential—a child in the house!

I shall get the Kings to you *somehow* on Wednesday. Don't worry if they are a bit late in the day—after all, it's a long journey from the Orient! But they will come.

God bless you, and I do thank Him for your friendship.

THE KITCHMORGUE
2ND FEBRUARY, 1943

… I do not attribute *any* of your conversion to myself in *any* way—but I rejoice in it as a glorious fact, and I am sure you won't lose your faith, because you will pray to keep it: and I shall also pray daily that we shall all keep our faith. I always have that sense of the danger too, and I often think of Our Lord saying to St. Peter: "Satan has desired to have you that he might sift you like wheat, but I have prayed for you that your faith shall not fail." Every Mass is Christ praying for *us* that our faith shall not fail. I think the time may come after the war when we shall realize more than ever how much we need that prayer of Christ's.

What you said about Christ's work and about the joy of *having* a "work" at all was a real light to me, Archie: truths, anyhow the last, that had never struck me. You know, you made me take a grip on my work and realize that it is worth any suffering on earth to hang on to it, and *any* effort to do it. Thank you for it.…

[†] Mrs. Campbell-Murdoch's daughter by a former marriage.

17TH JUNE, 1943

I think with you that there is nothing vital in the Russian Church which cannot be found in the Catholic Church. Clearly the mystical and charitable elements that the Russians stress almost exclusively, in a way—clearly they are to be found in Catholic mysticism and practice. But there is of course a difference of temperament between the East and West, and, viewed superficially, this would seem to make a great difference between the Russian Church and ourselves. This is completely exploded however, by the fact that Russian Catholics belonging to the Russian rite of the Catholic Church, and in every way the same Church as we are, are, so far as temperament and spirituality and liturgical practice go, identical with the Russian Church.

It is rare for the members of any religious body to get below the skin where any other religious body is concerned. They judge of them by a few people, usually not known intimately, and by their ceremonies.

I remember attending some Salvationist meetings once, and for a long time I was satisfied that I perfectly understood the Salvation Army; I had read some of their books and been to a few meetings! Later on I got to know one or two of them, including a very cultured man who was one of the heads, and I soon realized that I knew very little indeed about them and that it would take a lifetime to know a *lot* about any handful of human beings.

This superficial knowledge of one another causes the Russian Church people to be shocked at what they consider the irreverence of Low Mass; they find it a rush and a scramble, and that everyone at it behaves in an openly hurried and distracted fashion. It so shocks them to see any service spoken quickly, and lasting less than two hours, that it takes very long and a lot of patience to convince a Russian of how much more consistent with *his* devotion to the indwelling Christ it is to go to daily Communion (even in a hurry) than to refuse to go at all unless one has half the day free to spend in church.

I am absolutely in sympathy with the Russian attitude myself, and, owing to the love I have for them and to the astonishing generosity and trouble with which Mr. St. George has kept me fed on Russian spiritual literature, I know a bit about them and can lend you more stuff. My interest is frankly devotional, not controversial, and I use their writing not to aid me in argument but to aid me in prayer....

4TH SEPTEMBER, 1943
LUNCH HOUR: WORK

... Directly you return I want to keep the feast of your first birthday, though it will be a bit late—the 12th is the day, is it not? Well, we must appoint a day as soon as you return, and use it to celebrate both your and Sheila's birthday into the Church.

If I were you I would not let worries about motives and "pride," etc., worry me. Of course I know such worries try to intrude, but the more one works at them, the worse they get. If you contemplate Christ, keep your eyes fixed on Him, you will forget such worries, and you will realize that in any case being a saint is just one of His gifts. If it *is* given to you it's not something to be proud of, but it *is* something to thank Him for. As for wanting to be it, naturally you want to be whatever He wants you to be, and there is no pride in that, though there would be in wanting to be anything else. I am sure it's the devil who tempts good people with these sort of worries, for they distract from the quiet, loving attention fixed upon God which is the one thing the devil hates—and with reason! ...

005 NELL GWYNN HOUSE
13TH SEPTEMBER, 1943

Thank you very, very much for that lovely, solid block of chocolate, which has given us all the greatest possible satisfaction, and added to the sense of a feast day, just as bananas on the breakfast table did at my French convent. Those bananas had a kind of joyfully holy atmosphere, and were given to us only on First Communion days. Whenever I hear of the "heavenly breakfast" or "marriage feast of the Lamb," I always think of small girls dressed as brides, sitting in a row eating bananas—and now I shall see slabs of chocolate too....

I'm glad you mention Our Lady's birthday: it always seems a very special day to me. This year I appointed a little girl, one of my and Dr. Strauss's brats,[†] to be deputy for Our Lady, and I gave her the present, a nice dress, and a treat. The treat couldn't be done on the day, but is taking place next Saturday. It may be the ballet, but may descend to Madame Tussaud's. She has never seen either or *anything*, and the ballet hasn't even occurred to her; but she yearns for the Chamber of Horrors. I'm sure I don't know what view Our Lady would take of *that*....

Yes, I have read *A Diary of My Times* [*Les grands cimetières sous la lune* (*The Great Cemeteries Under the Moon*)], and I should strongly advise you not to read it. It is about the Spanish Civil War, very bitter against Franco: so far as I was concerned it only confirmed what I had heard before and believed, and I am a whole-hearted admirer of Bernanos, but I have always loathed Franco, because I have always believed that he tried to impose Catholicism *by force*, which is obviously a really un-Catholic, because un-Christian, thing to do. However, one can have very little certainty, if any.

But the fact is that, whether or not Franco does abuse his position, and whether or not there are or were abuses of, or by, members of the Church in Spain, you can do no good by reading about them. There might be a good object in doing so, if by so doing you could change them, but you can't. Again, I would advise some people to do so, people who would be interested without being upset—and there are many reasons why it is well to know what one can about everything concerning the Church and human beings and so on; but this does not mean that it is *always*, in every case, advisable for each individual to do violence to themselves by reading books likely to raise storms in their particular mind. You must remember that you have only time and energy to read a

---

[†] Dr. Strauss was a distinguished English psychiatrist and author, especially skillful with neurotic children. With some of these he asked Caryll to help.

certain number of books in your life, therefore each one you do read is a choice: it is read *instead* of another. This being so, it is wise to choose ones most likely to increase your consciousness of the presence of God, and ones most likely to enter into your mind and to enrich it for ever. I think for *you* this is particularly the case. You have wrestled with controversial matters with great courage, and it has been a grace—a grace to which you responded; but I do really think that if, for a year or two, you read some of those great books about God which teach the soul to rest in Him, you would afterwards find that you view hard, controversial matters much more easily. When I say, "rest in Him," I don't mean any sort of complacency or any sort of cessation of activity or activity of mind, but a rest like the rest in the wings of a bird spread upon and abandoned to the current of a great wind, swifter and stronger than its own flight.

The way I look upon the abuses and so on which inevitably crop up in the visible Church is that they are necessary, because they are the Passion. You see, the Church *is Christ*, and therefore Christ's Passion *must* go on in the Church. Tragic, even frightening though it is, we know Christ better with the kiss of Judas on His face.

But how to stand, what could be the bleak misery of that, and to know the glory in it as well as the tragedy? There is a problem, and if you don't solve it, it breaks you.

I am sure the solution is to abandon yourself to the contemplation of the love and beauty of God, to the mystery of the Trinity, to the unutterable bliss of the indwelling of the Holy Spirit; because if you do allow your soul to be swept along on this great storm-wind of love, like the bird with spread wings, you will find that one day you can look upon the face of the Passion, on what is ugly and confusing in the world, without faltering and with an increase of compassion for God and man.

30TH MAY, 1944

… Yes, I know something of workhouse life, as I used to go a lot to visit an old Russian man in Poplar workhouse. Yes it is a wretched and inhuman business, even when run by good kind people. The system is so inhuman in itself: for instance, separating old married people who have lived their lives together; and the ones where I went had nothing at all to do. They depended on charity from outside for anything at all in the nature of materials for hobbies, or for books to read, and many of them never got either. They just sat all day long, staring. The rooms themselves were like what I should imagine a prison to be. There was absolutely no sort of beauty of any description. Privacy does not exist, and if anyone has a guest, they must talk before everyone. I never slept after I had been there, so haunting was the sense of final despair there—and I was too cowardly to visit the really sinister rooms. One of them, I was told, was for deranged women, who were in separate cubicles with bars like cages in front of them. I never had the courage to investigate.

As to what can be done, the *only* thing, I think, that would really change this state of affairs would be the conversion of England. No amount of reform outside of that would really help, because it is only when everyone *sees* Christ in the poor and old and helpless that they are humanly treated. You see, this problem raises *all* the whole question of our interrelationship, and unless that is consciously based on a *real* belief in our oneness in Christ, there is no hope of the *complete* change of the whole system which alone can help. That is why I think lay apostleship must take the form of putting the Faith *entire* before people as far as possible.

Gestapo Headquarters
Lunch Hour

My dear Both, Archie and Sheila—or ought I to reverse it and say Sheila and Archie? Anyway, both. This is an, alas, *belated* note, to thank you both for your wonderful gifts, living buds and brandy. I don't think I thanked Archie half enough. Brandy is like running gold, as you know, and I felt we *ought* to have insisted on Archie taking back the part we did not drink, but, thank God, people don't *always* do as they ought to, and so faint-hearted was Iris's suggestion that he should take it back that it seemed to me a ready excuse for my own concupiscence in not backing up the suggestion. When I told them at the office about the lovely chestnut buds, they all wanted them, so after having selected the very best for myself, I divided the others among them, and it was good to see the poor old girls going off home, their faded cheeks glowing, and branches of sleeping life in their hands. How wonderful they are, dear Both, those branches of sleeping life; what more apt for our Advent meditation than to sit and look at them and to allow all that they are a symbol of simply to enter one's consciousness like sunlight and warm it to gratitude?

Speaking of gratitude: to feel grateful is, I think, one of God's great graces, and you Both are singularly blessed in the power you have of making people feel grateful....

30TH NOVEMBER, 1944

... I am glad that Gemma Galgani does not repulse you. All that she stands for is magnificent, and I personally am not revolted either by phenomena, marvels or extremes—just the opposite. At one time I was quite crazy on her, but in later years I'm afraid I have found her personally most unattractive. Mind you, as the Church has canonized her, I naturally accept and presume that my aversion to certain things about her is wrong and based perhaps on prejudices, etc., of my own. And then I can't help associating her type of spirituality with a great many pious women whom I have known well and who are not saints, but who go in for a well-nigh maniacal cultivation of their own souls—which to my, probably sinful, mind seems to be the most humourless egoism. It is usually accompanied by an ever-increasing insensitivity to other people and an ignoring of plain obligation, such as to parents, and a kind of horrid callousness to friends. I am bound to say I can't like it at all, and those cultivators of perfection really do seem (to me) to do what we so hotly deny, when accused of it by non-Catholics, i.e. put a priest above their own conscience, and dote on him to the point of insanity!

But oh, I am all for the pure gold, to show us Christ's values again, when we see it in the true saints; and I can still love Gemma as I did of old, when I forget her utterances, etc., and think of her, as I said that night when we discussed her here, as "another Christ," wrestling with eternal justice for the wounded world, and herself bearing Christ's wounds.

R. sent me a pamphlet about St. Joseph Labre, and it has a photo of his grave on the cover. This grave is the carved image of himself, and it is simply lovely. I was so moved by it—it seems to show the unutterable beauty of being emptied out for God. I must show it to you. Many people dislike him, and I can understand why they do, but I have always loved him and hope always shall. I think *every* saint, if one really thinks hard about them, is a little revelation of Christ and throws light on the real meaning, in practical life, of the solidarity of Christians in the Mystical Body. I do think that the very great and crying need in our day, for Catholics too, is a greater understanding of the Mystical Body.…

26TH DECEMBER, 1944

… I thought of, and of course prayed for, you at Midnight Mass. It's strange to think that, although Christ is eternal (a fact, I think, which makes it seem slightly strange to wish Him a happy birthday), Christ in His Mystical Body, in mankind, *is* actually entering on His two thousand forty-fifth year, and one can wonder and hope about this new year of Christ-life in the world, as really as one does about a new year in the life of a child or friend.…

24TH DECEMBER, 1945

… Now the next thing is about the idea for backward boys—I think it is a really superb idea, and that it is intended by God for you. I think that, because everything has led up to it; as if all your actions, buying the house and so on were (as I feel sure they are) part of a pre-ordained plan. I think, if I may be frank, that you should disabuse your mind completely of the idea that an action or way of life loses its supernatural value because it is a means to your livelihood, because you are paid. The idea that only unpaid work is real charity (love) is simply a snobbish idea which grew fat under the Victorian worldliness; it is not the Catholic idea. To start with, the idea is that everyone should *work*, and that their work, which ought to occupy most of their life and all their best energy and ability, should be in *itself* the chief means by which they give glory to God—that means that their whole-time job should be their holiest and most charitable self-offering. If they are not able to find work that fulfils that ideal, they are crippled all their life long.

To say that charity is *only* what is not paid for, and not a means to living, is the same as saying that the only people who can *fill* their lives with charity are the rich—the few exceptions, to be pitied, who need not earn their living; or alternatively that the poor and the huge majority who do have to work can only really glorify God in their spare time and when, in all likelihood, they are tired out and have only a fifth best to offer. Our Lord says, even in respect to the work of being Apostles, "The labourer is worthy of his hire," and He specifically told His Apostles to accept board and lodging in return for their apostleship. He Himself was a workman, and He did not give away the things He made; He took pay for them and helped to support His home and family.

One fulfils the ideal which Our Lord professed for Himself by humbly accepting one's pay for good work. "I come among you as a servant." One's work ought to be a service to humanity, we all ought to be one another's servants and, in humility and communion with one another, be glad of our interdependence and mutual poverty, which does so much to make life easier for everyone.... The idea of working for nothing does all too often become what the word "charity" has come to mean in the popular mind—not what it really means, and should mean, "love."

So I do hope you will forget all this snobbishness; you must see for yourself that if you charge a fair and reasonable fee for your little boys, that makes it easy for the parents to take advantage of your home. If they had to come free, the most sensitive ones would feel too awkward to come, and if they did so, they would likely enough feel humiliated, and that feeling would inevitably be sensed and assimilated by the child himself and do him lifelong harm.

You could, in the case of very poor parents, charge very little, and not let anyone know it, but in general a fair price is the most just *and the most kind.*…

Private enterprise in trade is in the melting pot; no one can see what conditions will be, and I have learnt that since the war several existing small bookshops have had to close. It was a great dream, and one side of it, I am sure, will come about one day, but if I were you I should put it out of your mind (I take full blame for putting it into it) for the present, and go all out on the little backward boys. I can't imagine any more lovely way of serving Our Lord in His members—each child will come into your house as the Divine Child coming into it, and that will make the tremendous patience that will be demanded of you blessed and sanctifying.

I have an idea which I will carry out if you like. Dr. Strauss gets backward boys brought to him—rich ones to Wimpole Street, poor ones to Bart's—and I know he is always in despair for anywhere to send the Catholic ones. How would it be if I told him about you and asked him to send some to you? I should, of course, make it clear that you can only take *backward* boys, not abnormal or delinquent ones, for they don't mix, and that you can't carry out any medical treatment. He might send you a good few, and again, he might sometimes ask you to take a really poor delicate child for a holiday now and then. At all events, you would have to go and see Strauss and have a talk, for he would have to have actually met you. He is keenly interested in music and I am sure you would like one another.

He keeps threatening me with invitations to dinner; it would be a great relief to write and say I won't come but my friend Archie will! But do go on with the idea; it is a very lovely one. I think, if you do it, you ought to pay fairly frequent visits to London, go to shows, etc. (cheap seats if you like!), also concerts, picture exhibitions, and meet friends (like me and also more intelligent ones), because, being all the time with

… the little dull boys (dull-witted, I mean) is bound to cramp and narrow your mind if you do not take practical measures to stop it. To serve children you want to get bigger and bigger in mind and heart and sympathy; they are all growing creatures, and you must always be growing too, to be able to serve them—and your temperament is apt to get constricted if you don't get some relaxation in a very occasional objective activity for your mind. Also you need, in order to give your best to boys or girls, to get *right away* from them every now and then. By the same token, Archie, and *please* forgive me if I am preaching and being odious, but for a long time I've wanted to write this: you *must* get over the idea that it is wrong to delight in things like flowers and cats. God created the beauties of the world as signs of His love, He gives you stars as a lover gives his beloved gems, He throws flowers down under your feet as a lovely quixotic gesture of His divine folly and extravagance of love, He makes them look and feel and smell lovely, so that through every sense you have got He will press His suit on you. Not to rejoice in such advances of heavenly love is black ingratitude; every petal that opens on a rose in your garden should be for you a fling of the heart to God. As to animals, they were only created to add to your happiness. It is true that now and then some pathetic frustrated old woman lets all her maternal instinct run amok on a cat (i.e. me and Jones!), but on the whole even *that*, though irritating, is harmless, and loving animals does not make us love other people less, but *more*. All love, all pity and tenderness, enlarges, warms and refines the heart. These little creatures are given to us to [help us to] love more, and as our capacity grows, even if it only grows through a humble little cat, we can take in more and more people. Every time you frustrate a natural and spontaneous feeling or expression of love, for anyone or anything, man, bird, beast or flower, you ultimately lessen your power of loving God.

Of course, I am aware that you have as an individual a "vocation" to a life of reparation, but you can find ways of satisfying that which do not include saying No to any love or joy that God offers you—such refusals are just snubs to the divine Lover. Above all, you owe it, or will do, to your little boys to fill your heart with all kinds of delights and funny things and beauties—once again, you can't give except by taking.…

Oh—here is a bit of egotistical news, which will amuse you: I have had a "fan" letter from Monsignor Ronald Knox about *The Reed of God*—only it is not "fan" in the vulgar sense; it's an incredibly humble and moving little note, which must have been inspired by perfectly *enormous kindness* and graciousness and makes one feel less than a farthing....

13TH MAY, 1941
(*After the doctor forbade her to continue giving lessons.*)

... I feel terribly sad myself about not coming down on Tuesdays any more: it is a real sort of nostalgia. I always knew that I loved the school and everything that it stood for: I used to *realize* that, every time I came and every minute I spent there; and I shall indeed come to see you all as soon as I can and as often as I can, without feeling too guilty about forcing myself on a desperately busy man.

My *great* consolation is that I am more and more sure that, with the good craftsmen you have got, who can give far more time and energy to the job than I could, and are quite certain to be better teachers, the boys will really get the sort of thing they need, and the improvement will be immediate and wonderful. I don't say this to provoke flattering contradictions. I had, and have, a very clear vision of what I dreamed of your doing there, but for many months I haven't had the physical energy to do much towards bringing it about, and I would not have had it either, even had I been living there. Also I haven't, and never had, the skill that could make my dreams become reality. I am by nature a person to start things, to sow seeds as it were; it requires others to see them through. Everything you tell me about your staff suggests that the ideal people *have* come along now, and I rejoice in the hope. Very likely all that has ever happened to them, to you, and to me, their sad and limiting experiences and so on, has led up to the great work they are going to do, and are doing, with you there....

VI

A Note on Incompatibility in Marriage

1.

... As to you, I have thought and prayed a great deal. I feel quite desperately sorry for you, and it hardly seems possible for you to go on trying to live with your husband, feeling as you do. Mercifully he has been at home so little that probably a definite separation would not give your little girl any sense of the break-up of her home. That always seems unforgivable to me—that parents should shatter their children's sense of security by suddenly robbing them of their home.... But if there has never been a home with both parents in it, there would not be any real change for [her].

I have been visiting a number of convents lately...and I have formed the opinion that it isn't nuns as such that are wrong with Catholic education, but fashionable nuns; take this one step back, and we get "good families." It isn't the Catholic attitude but the attitude of the rich, protected child of the rich, protected parents that is disastrous. The non-fashionable nuns...are as understanding about sex as *any* school mistresses ever could be—more so than the lay ones who have not had to discipline their thoughts and so have grown repressions like fungi; and they give children that essential for any hope of happiness in the world as it is, i.e. the poetry and inner meaning of our Faith. Also the non-fashionable convents have non-Catholics as well as Catholics, which is such an advantage. The fact is that there is a "caste" in the Church—the fashionable Old Catholic Family—and that's what one wants to break away from—not the Church. I am willing to guess that most of the Catholic neurotics belong to this caste! ...

2.

... I do feel desperately sorry for you...unhappily there are only a few priests who are able to feel compassion for us poor devils when we have to do the right thing, which is usually so utterly hateful to our tormented and twisted human nature. Also, in some cases—all, probably; yours, certainly—right is not just so simple. If, after praying and trying in earnest to make a good job of your marriage, you still find that the only result is that you are really getting to hate your husband, or to feel as if you do, owing to the constant aggravation of his presence, I should have thought that some compromise in the way of a separation would be the way to cause the least sin and misery to all in the end. I may be immoral to say this, but I can't think that a situation which you have struggled and prayed to make tolerable, in vain, and which does really lead to loathing, can be endured indefinitely. I know that marriage is binding and you are vowed and bound before God, and no amount of human pity and grief can make one say that vows before God, and sacramental unity, don't count: they *do* count and can't be broken with impunity; but all the same, if what you are bound to do is to love and honour each other, and if it has come to such a pass that together you can only hate and dishonour each other—surely it would give a better chance of preserving some kindness, at least, which would enable you to help each other later, if you remained apart for some time now? Of course, you would be bound to a life of celibacy, and if you, being weak, should slip off the carpet, you ought to realize it's a sin, and one that can't be rationalized because it's good for your nerves—or so you imagine—any more than it would be *right* (and not merely nice) for a repressed old maid like myself to alternate between bouts of fervour and bouts of too much gin, to relieve nervous tension! Sometimes, in this land of heroes, the aridity both for fervour and for gin is equal! …

I will write to you again, a more considered letter. But don't let me lead you astray. Remember, my dear, I give advice that is rather more human and sympathetic than orthodox, and I not only temper the wind to the shorn lamb but also to the neurotic sheep, whose need seems greater. But the root reason is that I *dare* not give unctuous and rigid counsel to anyone, because I am so profoundly and always conscious of being a sinner myself, not in imagination but in reality and with a ghastly accumulation of irrefutable proof. Consequently I *dare* not say to people, "You must do this or that because it is right," knowing full well that if I were in their shoes I would do something very much *more* wrong than they would.

Now God bless you and support you, and above all deliver you from this dilemma. Tell Him He *must*: point out to Him that though you want to do His will, you are a weak human creature, and every step of the way is on sharp stones; but He is all-powerful and can do whatever He likes, with no effort at all, and so let Him help you now!

3.

Thank you very much for your letter. I loved seeing you and you did me good—you have such real courage and integrity *and* charity.

I'm glad you have a plan: it helps, I think. Personally, although I see how essential it is to trust, I much prefer to trust that by a divine fluke my own ideas may work—they never do! I feel certain St. Teresa is working hard for you; I don't see how she could help herself. I shall pray every day for you, and look forward to hearing from you.

My anti-obsession exercise is working in my case. One or two breakdowns in charity have let in misery like a swarm of rats, but on the whole the disciplined tongue and the nightly exercise against obsession have led to some little beginning of peace. I hope you have found this too.

I do realize that because you do really love God, your suffering, bitter though it is, is healing the world's sorrow. Don't think of it in terms of what is unbearable to you, but when a specially bad hour ends, even in sheer weariness, think, "That is a drink of water to someone dying of thirst," or, "That is a bar of chocolate for a hungry child." It's mysterious but true.

The [other] situation is unchanged, but of course we don't know what's brewing in heaven!

… It is much better for you to make as clean a break as you can… I think, and I am glad you have. You have done all you possibly could to make your marriage happy, and clearly it is impossible for you and him to be happy together. It is very sad for you both—in fact, a tragedy—but it might be a very much worse tragedy in the end if you tried to force yourself to go on, and ended up by a real nervous hatred. Possibly in the far distant future you may be able to be much more to one another than you can now imagine. The best thing is that, although you have suffered deeply and been madly irritated, you have never allowed any venom to enter your feelings, or any bitterness; in fact, you have been motivated wholly by affection and humanity, and God will bless you for that and will bring you happiness.

I would not worry over leading a useful life; there is nothing better or as good as bringing up your child and giving her the best possible chance for her soul. People who are, or think they are, useful, with a capital U, are a real menace; they usually wreck the lives of every sensitive person for miles. One ought not to be useful, only just human and spiritually beautiful. God can fix things if we just become pliant and easy-going and don't try to do His job *instead* of Him.…

VII

To Henry Tayler (1940–1950)

This wartime correspondence is the most illuminating I have seen of Caryll's own life and feelings during the war. As told in Caryll Houselander: Divine Eccentric, *this friendship had begun several years earlier, but no pre-war letters have survived.*

Now Henry Tayler was a Catholic, one of Caryll's most intimate friends, sharing especially in those refreshments and relaxations which alone made it possible to keep sane under the Blitz: music, books, flowers—and above all the meeting of friends, with the rare physical accompaniment of agreeable food or a bottle of wine. One becomes aware in these letters of an atmosphere of mutual help making it possible to endure the unendurable.

27TH DECEMBER, 1940

I hope you have had a happy Christmas and are feeling much better for being by the sea and in beautiful country. I enjoyed it much more than I expected to; in fact, it turned out to be one of the happiest Christmases that I have known in grown-up life. I went to the "Midnight" Mass on Christmas Eve at the little church in Warwick Street (in Soho, just behind Regent Street) at one o'clock.† In other times one usually saw a lot of Italians there; this time not, but there was one—a very small, thin, rather dirty, black-eyed little boy acolyte, who looked as if he were the last Italian child in the world, or like the little lame boy left behind by the Pied Piper of Hamelin in a childless city. This child carried the statue of the Infant Jesus to the crib; he led the procession, and the procession consisted of himself, two old priests—one *very* old (and incidentally a widower with nine children!)—several soldiers carrying candles, and an enormous Negro with a tiny bunch of flowers in a huge black hand! It was most moving, and the church was filled with burning candles and scarlet camellias, which was so glowing and so in contrast to the greyness, the ruins, the cynicism and the tears outside that it made one feel as if one was literally *inside* the heart of Christ.

We spent Christmas morning opening our presents and at 12 o'clock went to the F.A. [First Aid] Post, where we had an astonishing lunch—turkey, plum pudding, trifle, chocolates, lemonade and crackers, all for 2d. a head—yes, I really mean twopence!

The most blessed moment was somewhere between lunch and tea, when it came to me as a sort of inward certainty that neither side would do any bombing. Even if, as may be so, the motives for this restraint were not so pure and idealistic as one likes to hope, the fact that, however mixed and tangled the motives, the fact of Christ's birth should have power to control the cruelty and fear of the nations, even for forty-eight hours, was so wonderful, it gave one hope for the world: man after all has great good in him, and there *can* be peace on earth. We had a very nice tea, and were not expected to play games, happily. We had a Christmas tree and lots of candles on the table, and it was not even, as one had expected, a total hen party; there were several doctors, the husband of "Sister," who is a policeman who is much too sensitive to arrest anyone! and who intends to be a fruit farmer after the war—and a sailor, brother of the musical clerk, a very nice young Jew, who is a

---

† During the blackout, Midnight Mass at midnight was not possible, so it was anticipated on Christmas Eve.

musician himself, and with him a Polish sailor with a hideous face and tremendous charm.

... I have put your little wooden crib out; it is on a beautiful, softly coloured, red silk handkerchief with orange candles on each side, and behind it, like a little flowering tree, some white freesias and a spray of the winter jasmine which is now blooming in our garden at Milborne Grove. It is all round Our Lady, covering her shoulders in sprays and spurts of glittering gold.

That experience when the bomb fell the other night was very queer. I knew of course that the raiders were right overhead but thought I'd try to get home; then I saw the thing coming—it was a land-mine and they shot it in the air. I thought, as one does, that it was coming at me—it seemed a certainty, but somehow just an ordinary thing to happen; then suddenly the whole sky went a dull cruel crimson. I thought, "I'd better get down on the ground," and the one thing that troubled me was that I was afraid of dropping some of your Christmas presents which I was still carrying. It must have been only a few seconds, but seemed like years, as I was able to *think* so calmly and clearly about not one thing alone, but several, and also about several people—and not in turn, one after the other, but all together, as if each train of thought ran along in a parallel line beside the other: it was an absolute example of how different time is to what we generally imagine. Anyhow, down I got on my face—the proper place for a creature to be before God, anyway— and suddenly I thought that the whole town was full of ringing bells; next, ARP men and rescue workers just seemed to rise up miraculously from nowhere and simply refused to believe I was not dead, as I was in a veritable sea of plate glass, *all* the shop windows having fallen out all round me—they fell out from Sloane Square to the Town Hall, and you can imagine the blast when I tell you (and it's true) that though the mine actually fell on Ebury Bridge it broke windows in the Hyde Park Hotel! But actually I had not got even a fragment on me and did not get as much as a scratch....

9TH NOVEMBER, 1941

… I have had a slight blow—*all* my work on the way to America has been sunk. Of course, when one thinks of what the sinking of a ship must mean to those who have lost *people* in it, it seems absurd to mind at all about *things*. On the other hand, it gives one just a tiny realization of how war is opposed to all culture, spiritual and intellectual, and [how] tremendous a fight we will have to maintain within ourselves, if we are to keep the flame of heavenly love burning in our minds.

On the practical side, I have to begin again and do the whole lot for the second time, and it will be a frantic rush, for now they must be done in a few weeks, and as I have already had an answer from the Censorship telling me to call for the interview tomorrow, the two jobs may clash.

But still, one must learn patience and how to work hard.…

6TH DECEMBER, 1941

… There is only one thing I can say about the work [censoring letters]—namely, I find it more and more absorbing, and it seems to bring before my eyes all the wounds and anxieties and courage and pathetic joys of the people of the world. I am able to pray for each one, to offer sacrifices when that seems to be called for, to commend them all to God—I begin to imagine what it must be like to be a saint in heaven and to see all the pitiful prayers of the world passing through one's hands. I don't mean that I'm a saint, but that, as the stuff passes through my hands, I can pray for each one, taking the hope or grief or anxiety of each and offering it to God. It never occurred to me that this sort of continual prayer for people would arise out of this job; now I wonder it did not, for it is inevitable.

… I think more and more of St. Catherine's idea of keeping her soul and her love locked in a little "cell of self-knowledge"—such a cell in one's own soul means peace.… You have your own cell; you will have to keep it very carefully and do all you can, by prayer, to make it very strong and peaceful…the giving up of something precious is just like the breaking of the box of precious spikenard over Our Lord's feet by Mary Magdalene. The more you realize that the war is the Passion, that it is *Christ* suffering in this huge tortured humanity, and *His life* in them that gives them such power and courage in suffering, the more ready you are to pour out this precious spikenard for His burial, and the more certain you are that He must rise in human creatures again, even on this earth, with the sweetness of new life, a new dawn of day in the heart—a dawn sweet in its austerity, washed with tears shed in the night to a limpid simple purity such as men have never known before. We shall be glad in the end, if God gives us grace to be courageous and generous in the hour of His Passion—glad because, although we are just dirt, the fact of having given Him *something* precious in His hour of suffering will make it possible for us to look into His eyes when the light of His own new day shines from them in the face of the world.…

13TH JANUARY, 1942
LUNCH HOUR: WORK

… It's true I've just been at the limit of my endurance. I think the cold makes everything more tiring, and having to come to anchor after work and then go out and face another cold journey defeats me—that is the worst part of all about going to the hospital. This, however, wouldn't have kept me from coming to you, were it not that I felt that I must not risk getting ill, as now I just have to hold fast to my work, or shall I say "works"—and I hoped to be able to come on one of my days off, but Fr. Bliss sent an S.O.S. for a terrific bout of work, with the result that I *could* not get time. That is the real trouble, time.

Don't worry, I will not get ill—I'm sure of it. Ideas are pouring into my mind, everything that was puzzling through the years past becoming clear and illuminated, as if God just began to reveal all the secret beatitude that we ought to be aware of—and I am sure that I will be allowed the strength to write it, as it is meant for other people. It is not easy to write, just because it all seems so obvious: when I go to write I find I can't explain at all. It is like trying to teach drawing; one asks, "What on earth is there to learn?"

26TH MARCH, 1942

First of all, most joyful news—viz., I have got Easter Sunday off, and so we can have your birthday tea here on that day—it will be an incredibly lovely Easter, I'm sure. Only we'll just have to put some notice or other on the door asking not to be disturbed, for Sunday is a fatal day.... I honestly don't think we need feel guilty over it, because all these Sunday callers come simply to pass time—in fact, to waste and get rid of the most precious thing, of which one can't ever get enough to *use*, and there is only destruction in this frittering away of time.

It is vanity to say that any human being can go on indefinitely without the contacts that are *really* creative, and with *no* undisturbed, *unstolen* communion with [those] whom one loves. Deprived of this, one soon becomes impoverished and incapable of giving *anything* essential to other people.

Talking of giving—today I saw the mother of that little boy I'm taking on for Dr. Strauss. She is such a nice woman and rather pathetic; she says the boy adores music and wants to take it up, and that he gets furious with her because she won't play to him sometimes: you see, she is a hairdresser, works from 9 to 6, and is expected to keep up sparkling chatter all day with her customers, and then goes home and cooks dinner for her husband, son and another boy and a woman lodger who lives with them, and has the house to keep clean too, so that when the child asks for music she often feels too dead tired to even try to play.

Dr. Strauss is a genius and sees how art and music can be and *must* be used as the expressions of love, and I see more and more vividly how *we* could combine to use these things to heal minds and to "make straight the way of the Lord." I wish that you could find an interest in this child and help him musically; I realize all too well what a huge effort it is to add *anything* to lives as busy as ours must be now, but I do feel that it would be a marvellous thing for *you* and your music as well as the boy if you could help, and [the] strength it would give to your soul would compensate you a thousand times for the effort it would cost...

3RD APRIL, 1942
GOOD FRIDAY

... I tried to ring you up several times, but you were out—perhaps at the Holy Week services. I tried in particular to get you yesterday to tell you that I got the day off unexpectedly: I was delighted, and I decided to go to the Mass of the Presanctified at the Cathedral; I wanted to ask, if you were free, if you would like to come with me, but I did not strike lucky. I wasn't altogether sorry, because I thought that very likely you would prefer to make your Holy Week alone—with me there with you in spirit certainly, but bodily alone, and I was half inclined not to ring you for fear you agreed to come with me out of kindness, and it might break a week of recollection and real union with God. I know that once, and only once, in my life did I achieve the Holy Week services, all of them, all alone, and at the end I was exhausted, but had experienced a nearness to God which was indescribable and which I have never ceased to feel the goodness of....

Anyhow, Archie turned up and asked if by chance I was free on Good Friday, and he did meet me...he is so easy and so absorbed in God, it's more like having a rather puzzled angel beside one than a man!

However, I did have a distraction—i.e. wondering if you were by chance in the crowded Cathedral.... When I went up to kiss the cross, I was between two of the loveliest worshippers—one a *completely* black, curly-headed Negro, with eyes only distinguishable from his dark face because they did literally *glow* with love. He was a huge man, well over six foot and in khaki; and on the other side the tiniest little girl imaginable, about nine years old, white-faced and dressed in worn-out and shrunken clothes, and carrying in her arms another child, a boy about three years old, almost as big as herself and fast asleep. She carried him over her shoulder like a sack; his head came down to her waist, and he was snoring very softly, like a puppy, fast asleep, and remained so all through the little girl's struggle to kneel down with her burden to kiss the cross....

Iris had been baking a cake all day with I can't tell you what temperament—it smells delicious! …

I now have two patients of Dr. Strauss' coming to me, and great freedom allowed in the treatment of them. We've just got to work music into it—I know it's essential, and they will never be made complete human beings without it. You will be able to do great work through it; don't imagine you haven't got the initiative: you convince yourself that you can't "give," but that's just nonsense: think of all you have given and do give to me! Nothing is so frightening or so baffling as a twisted human mind, but if you realize that Christ will work through you, the fear dissolves and you can help. The thing is to *ask* Christ to act through you, and ask Him often, and think often of how unsparingly Christ gave Himself to people in need. You won't want to limit the amount you will let Him use *you*, after a few such meditations. You have such great understanding and tenderness, and if you will only believe that you can, with God's help, you will work miracles of healing! …

27TH APRIL, 1942
LUNCH HOUR

… When I got home yesterday, I made Iris go into the bathroom while I got the birthday table ready—I lit the candle, put your present and mine on, and a parcel that had come from our old maid Kathleen, then I turned on the gramophone (a record she likes, that I had got for her). She was delighted; of course the Baron had sent marvellous red roses, and besides that, from various sources we had blossoming branches and daffodils, violets and primroses. Every poor old servant and surviving mad governess we have ever had, had remembered and sent her cards....

Dr. Strauss has written to me in a very encouraging way about the work I'm doing for X. I find that, working for him, I am able to put into practice all my theories about psychology, and I have great hopes that from our poor little shed and this one strange, lovely boy, our wisdom school may really begin. X has a mind like a beautiful valley almost hidden by a dark and shadowy twilight; in that twilight one hears the sound of tears and yet finds rare and isolated flowers growing, and these flowers have a positively sparkling brilliance.

Another little boy is coming next week.

... I feel that they are *our* children, and that makes it a thousand times more vital to help them to find their integrity and stand on their own feet and leave us: if I had children of the flesh I would want them to do that, and that's what I want these to do too. What then will remain to us, as our children? Well, just what is twisted and awry in the soul of childhood today—*that* coming to us in one boy or girl after another, to go away whole, so that we can make our own the labour of helping that mind to a rebirth and afterwards, as Christ said, "rejoice that a man is born into the world." ...

17TH JUNE, 1942

... I had to go and register, and the place where I did it was miles away, and the time appointed between 1 and 2....

Speaking of registering, *that* reminded me of Our Lady. It is a moving thought that it was when *she* went to register, Our Lord was born.

A census of the people—just like ours today, and Our Lady (who by the bye could have asked to be exempt, as she was pregnant) having the wonderful humility and obedience to go, and to go a long cross-country journey in primitive conditions and about to give birth to her baby! ...

When I got there, there was a long line of poor old mothers, and I felt a bit ashamed of looking much younger, though of course we were all the same age, for obviously their hard lives had made them look older; and there they were, with dirty little kids in prams and clinging round their skirts, and not one of them at all martyred or gloomy but full of back-chat and chaff and giving their kids occasional whacks on the backside just to "learn 'em"—but it didn't.

There was one other woman, not married, a cripple, very white and sweet-faced and patient—as she needed to be, for we were made to wait outside the door for an hour without anything to sit on! Then I realized more than ever the amazing humility of Christ's birth—Our Lady going off to stand in a queue like that, and fill in a form, and having to wait about and do everything just as we do, and into such circumstances and on such an occasion, God being born into the world.

Well—surely, then, we can hope for a rebirth of love now? The circumstances are reproduced in detail, and certainly God's love has not changed!

The clerks who took down the facts did not know what the Censorship is, and seemed to think it was something pretty fishy anyway! …

I do hope you are well; now I know how difficult food is when alone, I can't help worrying over you. I feel inclined to give up the struggle and eat blotting paper! …

2ND NOVEMBER, 1942

It was so lovely to come home and find your letter. I was thinking about you such a lot, and wondering if the strange dark splendour of today, All Souls' day, had, so to speak, folded you to its heart as it did me. This morning in church it was almost dark, only the candles on the altar for light, and the coffin before the sanctuary looking very big and mysterious, almost invisible in darkness—it came home to me more than ever before that it is only the Church that gathers the living and the dead into one vast gesture of love; only she who weaves even the darkness of death with tenderness and splendour of everlasting life, and only, so to speak, in her lap, that the vows and loves and longings of little human creatures become immortal.

Without our faith, every relationship, every beauty, every hope, every discovery or "advance" of human nature is uncertain; looking back, one sees how they have been swept away, broken by trifles; one knows that all that we toil and strive for is as fragile as a spider's web, but the Church remains, and in her strong and tender hands human loves grow strong and bridge even death itself, and we are reminded of it more than ever today when every Mass is for the Holy Souls and we greet our dead friends one by one, with the certainty that they are so close that they are even sharing our heart-beat.

But really I must stop this rambling and get to the point of my letter—if any? I don't think there is any. But I was going to write again to thank you for X. I can't tell you how happy I am to see you doing such a wonderful thing for him; *he* is radiant about it.

I think his troubles are really psychological, but they are quite desperately real, my dear, and it would be wrong to let his lovely personality blind us to that fact. He is very weak, so easily led to folly in order to be like other boys—boys who can't hold a candle to him, too. We must have a talk about helping him; could you come to dinner with me on Saturday night? ...

28TH JUNE, 1943

... I will tell you frankly that I think the Home Guard one of the most moving and splendid things that have grown out of the war. The idea of its almost blind beginning—farmers with literally spades and rakes for weapons, clerks who gave themselves ungrudgingly after a hard day's work, men too old to fight, yet ready to fight and die, and boys too young—and there was never any fuss or side, or any worked-up patriotism; it was the real outward and visible sign of their inward love for their homes and families and friends, for their fields and the particular streets that mean their country to them—for in each man's soul, one street and one house and a handful of people are his country.

The big parade they had lately was the first "show" they ever gave, and it made one realize what the "brotherhood of man" means, and that it really *does* mean something—far more than all the things one has read and heard from the semi-intellectuals of the Left.

You know that I don't believe in one human being trying to exert too much influence over another in matters that affect their whole life, and I would never dream of even expressing too great enthusiasm when you mention the Home Guard, in case you thought I was trying to influence you to join it. But now you will probably have to do so, and I can see no harm in saying all I can to encourage you to do so with a whole heart.…

12TH OCTOBER, 1943

If you can, come before 4 o'clock on Saturday, because otherwise we shall have practically no time at all for records.…

Yes, we will have some Bach; I'll see what I've got and let you know; perhaps you could bring the Brandenberg if it's not here, but I rather think it is. You could take it away again on Sunday if you are going on to a guard duty; if it is an all-nighter you'd better go to Mass at the end of it—to the 6 o'clock one—and then go and spend Sunday in bed. I could come and get your tea! or, if you like to sleep till 4 o'clock and then get up and come here, I could prepare a nice war-time meal, tea and breakfast in one, to which we all seem to be introduced at one stage of the war or another.

My dear, did you think your uniform would fit? I've never yet seen an H.G. in one that did—and it is not the *smart* soldier idea that is so lovely about the Home Guard; it's just the fact that none of them *are* soldiers, but are poets and everything else who, for the love of home and friends, and without mawkishness…take upon themselves the ardours and endurances of soldiers, in the spirit in which Christ took upon Himself our human nature, to bear and share its burden.

I want to introduce you to Shane Leslie; he is also on Home Guard, and looks strange and yet so *right* in it. He is going to come and read poetry to us at Esmé's flat, which is in the Meynells' house in Palace Court....

Certainly if you've not had much music lately, we must have more here. I always listen to the music *before* the "Lift up Your Hearts" on the wireless; it's before the 8 o'clock news—do you listen? They take a different composer each week and give one or two of his things each morning, and you (if you are ignorant like me) get to know that composer. To me the week of sheer illumination was the Handel week. "Illumination" is the right word; each day it seemed that this music filled my soul, very gently and softly, with a soft but all-pervading light, and I went to work with a wonderful calm in my mind.

(Undated)

I'm writing to thank you for waiting in London to give X his lesson. I do realize that you have to make a sacrifice in giving up some hours of your weekend with your friends, and I would never have asked you to do that, were it not that the thing is so much more critical for him than I could explain on the telephone, although I know you understand well enough without explanation.

If the trouble I told you about had not just occurred, I should have let him take the disappointment; a boy of his age can take a lot without hurting, and they have to adjust themselves to life; but you see, most of his life has been crowded with suffering, discouragement, disappointment which no one has recognized—I can't tell the *whole* story because I have it in confidence—a professional confidence; but as you can understand, when all these troubles suddenly break out in misdeeds, those misdeeds are as glaring and public as the sadness and strain has been secret, and in the case of so sensitive a child the tendency is for him to lose heart utterly, condemn himself, say it's no use trying, and to imagine that everyone he admires will find out and shun him.

He is unusually gifted and has a very rare fineness of character, and with him a huge struggle is going on to keep alive the fine part—music, poetry and so on—in spite of all the enemies which assail them, both outside and, far deadlier, inside himself.

He has taken a huge liking to you and sees in you the fine sensitive side of life. Had I had to put off this *first* lesson, and *indefinitely* at this moment, it would really and truly have been quenching the smoking flax—a bruise to his soul which we might not have had skill to heal; for no matter what I said, he would have imagined it was some sort of shrinking from him, and that you knew about his late troubles and would never feel friendly to him again.

I don't exaggerate; with these children I suffer myself—you can't help them if you don't; to give all my spare time to them seems silly, but you have to (I mean I have to), and you have to share their sense of defeat, shame and so on, go with them step by step through the dark valleys and bring them out again to the light....

8TH JANUARY, 1944

I am always full of charming things that I am going to do, only they never come off. I was going to send a letter to be there waiting to greet you when you arrived, but I lost your address almost directly you had given it to me, and although I have had a wild search for it whenever I have five minutes to search in, I have only just found it....

I did not succeed in getting my Rhythms off on January 1st; in fact, I'm still typing them. I had an awful (in the sense of being pathetic) letter from Fr. Bliss imploring me for material.... Well, I realized that what I was really asked for was four drawings and four stories in two days! So I've been trying to do it: I did not do it in two days, in fact I have only done half of it now, but when it *is* done, I'll go on with my typing.

Pat Dunlop brought his brother Michael to tea with me. He is such a wonderful boy—Michael, I mean; he says that in case he loses his sight altogether he wants to look at really *beautiful* things—not pretty things, not a multitude of things, but some few things of incomparable beauty which will remain in his mind for ever. Imagine that from a kid of seventeen, faced with blindness! There is, however, hope that the blindness has been arrested and that, though he will never see better than he does now, he will not go totally blind.

Yesterday, in spite of Fr. Bliss, I upped and offed to spend your lovely book token—also, as Archie and you both gave me the same vol. of the *Summa*, I changed it for Vol. 5 (I could not get Vol. 4, they hadn't got it). Vol. 5, like Vol. 3, is about angels, and very lovely indeed by the look of it. I shall get Vol. 4 when they have it. With your token I got *Why I am a Jew* by Somebody Flegg: it's a wonderful book. And I ordered a new book of Anglo-Saxon poetry, reviewed in last week's *Sunday Times*: they had not got it, but I shall have it in about a week. You will be interested in it too; there were extracts from it in the review, which were most beautiful.

I want to get a Mass, or some sort of plain chant records, for you; they will be the beginning of the records for the shop. Do you know any nice ones? I would like to get a complete Mass, and keep it myself for a few days to get familiar with it, before I give it to you....

29TH MAY, 1944
OFFICE LUNCH HOUR
(END OF ONLY)

... I want to thank you again for the *Saint Augustine*; it seems to me the most significant present that I have ever had.... I can see that this translation is going to make him, or leave him, what he always was to me—a deeply loved and reverenced figure, too modern to be of the past, too much rapt in God, indeed, to be set in time at all, and yet so human that he is in *all* times—but this book makes him an even *more* close, intimate friend and guide in our own life. At last he speaks to us in our own tongue—and goodness, what *superb* English Frank uses, so direct and simple, with words that ring, but ring deeply and rhythmically; it's almost like Bach rung on a peal of golden bells—and by the way, absurd as it may seem, I *can* just imagine Bach, or some of him, played on great solemn bells....

Oxford
7th August, 1945

This is only a tiny note to prove to you that I still think of you when on holiday and in the midst of distraction and enjoyment. This is my holiday, though short: it started yesterday and ends today.

It is so beautiful here; the atmosphere is so sane, and everyone seems to be concerned with lasting things like philosophy, poetry and music, not with the tittle-tattle one is used to; and then one feels that ages on ages of quiet thought [have] entered into the very stones of the old buildings....

Archie dined until us last night. He is simply in his element; he has met countless priests—also devout and musical lay men and women, all the members of the Society of St. Gregory...musicians whose aim is to give the utmost glory to God in the Mass. It is for that reason that they try to perfect their singing. We went to Compline last night, which was sung by them—about a hundred of them, and they sang it very, very well....

I went to the Carmelite Convent: indeed, our object in coming at all was to fulfil a promise to Our Lady which we made during the Blitz, that we would give a silver star for the shrine of Our Lady of the Woods, if we were spared the bombs (I mean, spared from destruction by bombs).

Nell Gwynn
23rd December, 1945

... I have a note from Frank in which he expresses his wishes in a way which, coming from him especially, most gloriously dispels anxiety neurosis. He says: "This is to wish you a merry, even uproarious, if necessary disedifying Christmas."

... Yesterday I got an invitation which was really a command to go and see old Mrs. Mackail. She is, of course, the widow of old Dr. Mackail who printed "Philip Speaks," and she is the daughter of Burne-Jones. I think she is the last link with the Pre-Raphaelite School—a *most* beautiful person, and so serene and joyful, belonging to a different world. When you go into her house, it is as if you walked back into a different time—a time that is past. One felt the presence of death in the house, but not as something heavy—rather as light; and sorrow, but sorrow completely transformed by dignity, and a serenity and joy—joy of a kind that is untouchable by sorrow or change, and which is completely unimaginable to most of *our* generation with their joyless grab for pleasure....

What I wanted to say is, that going from such contrasting people, from one to another, gives me the sense of living in various ages—as if one did not simply go from one house to another, but from one period of time to another. When I returned from Mrs. Mackail I felt like a ghost...come back to a world in which I *could* not have any part, as if I was a dead person, a ghost!

31ST DECEMBER, 1947

... May God give you the joys which only He can give and which, when He does, no one and nothing can take away from you; and I hope that He will also give you in abundance the multitudinous little delights and pleasures and surprises which the world, alas, can and does take away, but which are delightful while they last, and to some extent made precious by their very uncertainty! ...

7TH JANUARY, 1948

The day for Clare's baptism has been fixed—Sunday the 18th at 3 o'clock at St. Mary's, Cadogan Street… I can't tell you how happy I am that you are going to be the godfather… I will get and send you the little book by Father Martindale explaining the ceremony of baptism, and I know that you will find it a most exquisite meditation. I read it for the first time when I was preparing to be godmother to Elizabeth (Dickie's baby), and that which lit up my mind at the time, and has remained as an inspiration ever since, was the realization that being a godparent means much more than taking a promise: it means representing, *being* that perfectly innocent child before God. It means that jaded and shop-soiled though we are, we are ourselves, as it were, made new in the shining water of baptism: the flame that is given in the ceremony for a symbol of faith is relit in our hearts, and we receive the white garment of chastity, not as ourselves, but as the little child. I have made it a practice to go to Confession and Communion every so often *as* my infant godchild, until she comes to the age of reason; to go on *being* her, until in the sacramental active life she has the use of reason and can be herself. This is like carrying a sinless child in one's heart always, and when one feels the burden of one's own beastliness heavy upon one, or is depressed and conscious of being old and disillusioned and very sere and yellow indeed, one always returns to the thought that one is not only oneself by oneself, but also a little new, untouched, untried, unspoilt child, whom God has given to one in trust. This is the beautiful inward life of being a godfather, and then there is the sterner side; until she is not only at the age of reason but independence, *you are her reason* and the flowering sword of her defence.

… The only prayer I've said for her (as being her prayer) up to date—and this she "says" by arm gestures every morning at 6 o'clock—is the little child's prayer made up by the poet Herrick, which is:

> *Here a little child I stand*
> *Heaving up my either hand.*
> *Cold as paddocks though they be,*
> *Yet I heave them up to Thee.*

... I shall expect you here, next Saturday afternoon. Come as early as you can; we might then get time to play "The Ceremony of the Carols" before the echo of the Christmas "Gloria" has quite died away.

I have been playing "The Hymn of Jesus" to myself on the now rare, and rarer and rarer, occasions when I am alone, and finding it a real inspiration. The more often I hear it, the more I love it.

21ST JUNE, 1948

... I had an incredible day at the Lunatic Asylum yesterday. Met several Queens—female ones—one, the "Queen of the Whole Earth" whose hand I was allowed to kiss and who conferred many titles upon me! Half, more than half, the lunatics are practically sane, except on one point, and some even go out to work every day. I've seldom, if ever, been present at anything so moving as the prayers in the tiny Catholic chapel in the evening, organized entirely by the patients, the prayers of their own choosing and said aloud: and what a mystery and what an example—an ex-Trappist monk, a young girl, an old lady bent double nearly, but in spite of it and of being insane, beautiful, and a handful of others—all people who had started out in life intent on a high vocation, and given it indeed—utter abnegation, put away in a lunatic asylum. And this is the point—they reached out in their prayers to the whole world. As I knelt among them, listening at first and in the end joining in unconsciously with them, I grew more and more amazed at their petitions:

"For Russia";
"For the suffering people of Europe";
"For the sick";
"For prisoners";
"For the conversion of the world";
"For purity of heart in the world";
"For purity of heart here"—

and then, to me the most moving petition of all, "That we here in this little chapel dedicated to Your divine Heart may have perfect abandonment to Your dear will."

Think of *my* grumbling petitions!

After all the petitions, and many more, there followed interminable litanies, and I must say I began to get a bit anxious, because it seemed the prayers were going on for ever: I began to wonder if I was once more taken in, and it was but another form of obsession. But no, it was simply an almost unbelievable showing of the heart of the Mystical Body of Christ, literally bleeding before God with the wounds of the world!

And all round this kind of buried little chapel (it seemed to be in the catacombs; it was in the basement), the world of the lunatic asylum was a visible close-up of what *is* happening in the world, but with all the masks and bandages off. A lunatic, one of the "displaced people," raving without cease; another (this made my blood run cold!), a martyred mother raving about her daughter in a padded cell: as to those who find immorality necessary to rid themselves of their biological inhibitions, I would advise them *not* to read books for sensitive neuropaths, but just to call at the asylum and see just what depravity looks like and feels like, face to face, when the guilt feeling has finally been liquidated!

I could go on for hours, but I must not; but it has opened my eyes to the very heart—almost to the answer—of the problem of evil. As to the matrons and nurses—well, you just see Christ on earth! …

1st June, 1949

… I am at present obliged to work late at night, until 2 or 3 in the morning, and without any energy at all, because darling little Clare is indeed a whole-time job, and an exhausting one. She requires continual washing—herself, her clothes, her bedding—and of course is at the *most* difficult age—has to be watched and prevented from smashing herself and everything else we possess to bits all the time, but she is worth everything one can give her in devotion and love. She is such a glorious little thing, and her character is developing as something quite lovely. I took her today to visit the Blessed Sacrament, the first time she has done so since she was baptized (unless she did so in Scotland, which I do not know). When she had toddled up to the sanctuary (a slow process, as she constantly returned to crawling and had to be picked up for a few more staggering steps), she stood on the step of the altar rail and to my amazement, as I had not told her to do so, she made the gestures I taught her to make for saying her grace.... It astonished me that she acted the only *prayer* she has ever been taught the moment she came up to the tabernacle.

She is *most* loving.... Of course when she is a little older, walks steadily, can talk and can begin to draw and look at picture books and so on, it will be much less tiring....

9TH MARCH, 1950

... I am afraid I shall be unable to come to you on Saturday, as you suggested, as I only got up yesterday (after a whole *month* in bed!), and I am not allowed to go out of doors, and it will be some time before I shall be able to go out after dark (i.e. return after the sun has gone down). I still have the blessed orders not to see anyone, too! This of course I should not carry out where you are concerned, but I am doing my utmost to do so in all other cases.

It has been wonderful to be alone and able to put all my energy into my book and none into the frittering away of life that one usually has to.

... I am incomparably better than I have been for months, and this altho' the inflammation in one lung is still hanging fire a little. I still have to have more treatment, but the wonderful thing is how the ability to enjoy beautiful things is simply flowing back into me. For more than a year my senses have been dead to beauty, and anything like music or even looking at a beautiful scene has only seemed to add to the effort of being alive almost unbearably, but I only realized how much this is so by the sudden wonder, like a miracle, of being moved and carried away the other evening by the voice of a Spanish woman singing on the wireless—a real Spanish voice, with that strange mixture of hardness and deep, deep warmth and love, a wonderful inconsistency that somehow seems logical in a Spaniard—a mixture of fire and water—if you can imagine the miracle of water burning—you find it in the writing and the mind of St. Teresa of Avila. To my amazement I was just carried away and came alive in the beauty of this singing, and ever since, everything—flowers, light, poetry—has touched something in me that could waken and respond, going out to meet the beauty with something in myself, instead of shrinking back from the effort of response, blinking at it, as a person with aching eyes blinks at a strong light.

Also my own mind is filling with words—rhythms, stories—and I am now burning with impatience to finish my book, and write just for the sheer joy of poetry, words, etc.

One thing this illness has taught to me; it has made me realize that though God has given me gifts, I have never in all my life, for one single week, been free to *enjoy* them. They have always been violated, scamped, hurried, fitted in to other people's convenience, and never allowed to grow. They might never have come to much in the way of art, and now they certainly won't, for I am too old, and, in spite of this little resurgence of life, too broken, to develop talents now, even *if* I ever could have. But one thing I am sure, they could come to great personal happiness, and they should do—that alone is a real thanksgiving to God, and now I am going to achieve that. What remains to me of life, I am going to live happily....

VIII

To a Friend About To Have an Illegitimate Baby

I have torn up the letter I started to you, because I do so hate disjointed letters; and now it is so late at night that I feel sure no one can break in—anyhow, if they try to, I won't let them! So now I can write to you about our child—I am being presumptive [sic] in calling it *our* child, but I know you will forgive me, as I just can't help feeling already a great pre-natal love for It (with a capital I, as we use reverently for the Blessed Sacrament).

First of all I want to thank you very much indeed, much more than I can find words to say, for asking me to be "Its" godmother. You know, I don't think that people always realize what a wonderful thing it is to be the godparent of a little child. It means, in a sense, taking the place of the little child before God, until It comes to the age of reason—being Its ambassador in heaven. One has to speak for the child, in a way to take the place of It at the baptism—but I think it goes long beyond that. Whenever I have a baby godchild, until It comes to the age of reason, I go the sacraments, Confession and Communion, for it. This sounds rather odd, as an infant cannot need to be absolved, but at all events it is a kind of rebirth for me, and it simplifies the "examination of conscience" wonderfully, because one approaches it in a child's spirit, and is somehow "born again" because of that child, at every Confession and Communion.

Enough of that—and myself!

It is wonderful to see a mother like you, one who realizes what it means to bring a child into the world! I mean that it is a kind of rebirth of Christ—yes, it really is that, although in cowardice one hardly dares to put these great miracles of God's love into words, and of course no words can really speak of them. But the fact is, no child can ever come into the world by accident, and no new life can ever be anything but a glory, because every human being has been planned, and predestined, and loved by God from all eternity; and planned and predestined to be what? To be Christ—"another Christ"—to come into the world as the Son of God, to redeem the world and to bring more love into it, love that will ultimately overcome all its suffering.

Never forget—indeed, I know you will not—that God is your child's Father; that before the world was created, this child was the Springbreak in the bosom of Eternal Love, the joy and delight of the Father, because to Him your child was always present, as if the world was created for him and for no one else, as His own Christ!

Everything, all through the ages, that has led to the birth of this child, his heredity, through you and through his natural father, has been something foreseen, allowed, in a sense arranged by God, his eternal Father; and what joy it must be to God, and to Our Lady, who shares the Motherhood of Christ with you, to see your courage and common sense in accepting this tremendous responsibility!

To come to rather mundane things, I forgot to tell you today that I have ordered your wool to be made up into bonnets, gloves, and possibly vests, according to how far it will go (quite a long way), and I have also ordered two "leggings" (with feet on) and two "pilches" from the blind people—all these things will soon be ready.

Is there anything else you want—how about a carry cot and the bedding for it? Shall we go together to get that? Or have you got that? No hurry anyway.

I also ordered *Common Sense in the Nursery*—a really excellent little Penguin book, for you, but it had not come when I called for it before you came this morning. I hope that I will have it before you come again.

You said in your letter to me how Our Lady must love your child, as she arranges everything for it so well; clearly she does, because for her, as it is for you, it is once more a Christ-bearing, but I think she must have a very special feeling for you, and a very special attitude of protection for both you and the child, because of the circumstances, which are actually outwardly like her own before the birth of her Son; she well knows what it is like to feel alone in the world and misunderstood, with what to St. Joseph seemed a fatherless child. I have what is almost a conviction that she will presently bring someone into your life whom you will love and who will be a real foster father to your child....

IX

To Christine Spender

Caryll's friendship with Christine Spender began during the war, when both were working in the Censorship, and continued throughout the rest of her life.

16TH AUGUST, 1945

... Well, the war is over! You may know this, however! But the point is that you know now that you have no longer any excuse for remaining at the office. I believe your extreme fatigue does come from the fact that you have been frustrating your creative energy for too long.

19TH, SUNDAY

There you are—I started this three days ago, only to be disturbed so often that I got no further than you see.

To return to the subject of your fatigue: I read, and I fully believe this, that creative artists of any sort can only renew their energy by using it in creative work, their art; that if they do not, it does not simply go into whatever they use (or do) instead of their proper work, but flickers out altogether; consequently, after some months of complete frustration of their art, they cease to have any energy. This is certainly what happened to me, and I think it is what is happening to you. I hope you now, at last, will be able to get to your own work.

You certainly have shown yourself to have a wonderful character and wonderful fortitude to have stuck the job for all these years, but now really it should be over.

... I am still struggling with friends and acquaintances, who will certainly never let me write if they can help it. When on the very extreme edge of madness, I made a firm stand and really stopped opening the door; for a few days the incessant knocking almost completed my madness, but I really think that they are losing heart, as for two days now there have been only one or two knocks at wide intervals.

I have become *engrossed* in the book I call my "novel." It is not really a novel—the subject is the suffering of innocents—but it is fiction. I don't know if it will ever be fit for publication, but I do know that I've *got* to write it, and the writing of it is teaching me an amazing number of things that I have no idea of when I pick up my pen to write!

I dreamt of your first kitten that died. I went up the slope of a mountain, a snowy mountain, and there on top, made of shining snow, with tiny wings springing from tufts of swans-down on his shoulders, was your kitten, dancing! He had ice-blue eyes....

27TH JANUARY, 1946

... I think you ought to write, and I think you ought to write whatever you want to. The only problem I can see for you is how to arrange your life in the best way to help you to do so. It is not at all the same problem as mine; mine was never—to write or not, or what to write: I always knew what I wanted to write and that I wanted to write more than to live—in fact I hope, and I mean this quite literally, that if anything does ever stop me writing, I shall cease to live: but my problem was how to live, how to get the money to eat while writing; and it never even entered my head as a possibility that my sort of writing could earn a living itself!

However, the problem now is how to discipline myself so that I do go on writing, when, as it does now, it depends simply on my own will; and it was because I imagined that this would be your problem too that I said it *might* be a good thing to have an office job, because that gives a sort of routine, which is to a certain extent a necessity. I never meant the office job to be the object of your life, but a means to an end, and not, for that reason, done any less wholeheartedly.

But obviously you know yourself how you best work. I find that my vitality is exhausted and that I can no longer cope both with people and with writing, and I am certain that for me the *real communion* with people is in writing, and this does not only apply to strangers but to my intimate friends; I have realized that when they keep me from writing, they are actually destroying all hope of communion between us. With you, however, it may be otherwise; social contact may be a necessary stimulus.

You see it's hopeless to judge by oneself....

I think that you, like me, instinctively feel that your work should and *must* be a communion with other people, and shrink from criticism because, by the attitude of criticism, even the most kind and helpful, a person sets themself *outside* of the work, detaches themself and becomes an outside observer: this makes communion through the work an impossibility. However, if one's work *is* to be a communion with humanity, then one has to suffer for it; one has to suffer seeing its imperfections, for one thing; after all, our work is ourself, and this being so, we can be certain that it will *never* be perfect. It is vanity that makes people prefer to destroy, hide and frustrate their work, rather than see its imperfection face to face. In life we have to learn the great lesson of forgiving ourselves, accepting ourselves as we are; and if our work is a true child of one's own being, the very same thing applies. But believe me, Christine, that is only the smallest of the sufferings involved in realizing the longing for one's work to be a communion with others.

One suffering involved is simply this giving of one's body, drop by drop, always driving on the will—until ultimately every hour of every day is a struggle against fatigue; and then knowing that even when it is done, one will very truly have to say, "Lord, I am an unprofitable servant," because there will always be so much left undone, so many people not seen, so many letters not answered, so many people hurt because one tried not to hurt anyone! …

2ND MARCH, 1946

… I was going to write to thank you again for *The Little Locksmith*[†] and to tell you that I have hardly ever in my life read anything which so relieved my own feelings and expressed them. It's not only what she says about her writing—which by the by so exactly expresses what I feel, that I can just show that chapter to people instead of trying in vain to explain to them—but her whole conquest. I must feel that I look as deformed as she really did, for though reading her makes me feel ashamed of it, I am *as* self-conscious about my looks—not looks only, but presence: perhaps even more so; she did realize that her true self was in her soul—and how radiant and wonderful *that* was!—but I feel that my soul is even worse than my body and every personal revelation an added indecency! But there is comfort and hope and strength in every line of that book, and the closing passages are *superb* writing—of course it's all lovely writing, though. She is also like many other people as well as me. I do thank you so much for all you've given to me in that book.

30TH APRIL, 1946

This is only a little note in which I have not time to say anything at all, and am only writing so that you will get it very early in your visit, and it

---

[†] By Katharine Butler Hathaway (Faber, 1944).

will, I hope, reduce the cut-off feeling. I also want to tell you that I will say a decade of the rosary for you at 12 o'clock every night while you are there, and I shall be very surprised indeed if Our Lady does not allay all your fears and give you quiet sleep. Don't you love the lines in "The Ancient Mariner"?

> *To Mary Queen the praise be given,*
> *She sent the gentle sleep from heaven,*
> *That slid into my soul.*

Do not have any fear, and remember that even if you do, God holds you in His hand in the midst of any fear. Hackneyed though it is (a fact which really only proves that it has comforted millions), I always derive immense peace from this quotation: "If I ascend into heaven thou art there; if I descend into hell, thou art present. If I take my wings early in the morning and dwell in the uttermost parts of the sea, even there also shall thy hand lead me and thy right hand shall hold me."

22ND султемвек, 1948

22ND SEPTEMBER, 1948

… I will ask you to tea as soon as I can, but now I have collapsed with some heart trouble (not a love affair! a physical disorder), have been ordered to see no one, write to no one, do nothing, for a month. I *can't* carry this out to the letter, but up to a point I must, as it has become literally impossible to exert myself. If I fail to be left alone here, I will be compelled to go to the cottage. I hope that if I keep strictly to orders for the next week or two, I may be so much better that I shall be able to write to ask you to come.…

I can't remember word for word what X said, but the gist of it was that you must acquire absolute abandonment to God through contemplation—give up all ambition and effort (even to write) and live (anyhow for a time) a life of simple obedience, practising daily union with God.

You can write and ask him if you like; say I am ill and unable to repeat his words as fully as I would like to in person, and have given you his address to communicate with. I don't know if he is allowed to write to you (he does not, to me), and, if you remember, he did refuse to advise you in person when he was here and I asked him to; but if you gave him your story and asked for just one letter of advice, maybe you'd get it. But take warning; if you do, it will be drastic....

1ST OCTOBER, 1948

... I think that you are right, and extraordinarily brave and honest, in accepting X's ideas about your life.

His belief about you was that you are meant to be a contemplative, and for this purpose to abandon yourself wholly to God and complete inward surrender. For that purpose to give up *striving* for any kind of success and, if necessary (he seemed to think it would be), to give up all effort even to write at all. He said that the amount of effort and anxiety you are putting into trying to write is only frustrating you; that if you abandon it all into God's hands and make no effort to do anything else but to unite yourself to God, He will give you what you are to write, if He wants you to, when He wants you to; and if that happens, the writing you will then do will be done without effort at all. Your preoccupation with form and what you suppose to be perfecting your craft, he said was all wrong, and was in some (very complicated) way connected with an unadmitted wish to emulate your brother,[†] which is full of unrest, and can only be got rid of by giving up writing at all, until this effortless flow suddenly comes to you (if it does!).

He also said you should give up all conscious effort to do good or kind deeds on a big scale, or any scale, and find a wise person, not necessarily, though preferably, a priest, who would direct you—not so much in things like prayer, but by giving you a daily programme,

---

[†] The poet, Stephen Spender.

mapped out, containing small acts of love and humility and very humble jobs to be done and finished. You should not, he said, during this time of healing, make even simple decisions from hour to hour, as making decisions wastes energy for you. Even such things as going out for a walk to be decided in advance for you. After a time, you would find yourself suddenly at peace, and then if God wants you to write, or do something, you will know for certain what it is, and do it without effort and well. I said, "This is surely very drastic; I shan't be able to bring myself to tell it to her, even. *I* could not take it." To which he replied, "Yes, of course it is drastic, but she is a drastic person with a drastic vocation; that is just why a drastic remedy alone can bring her peace, and why she will continue to be broken by her resistance to her vocation."

Let me add, as a warning, that no one could be more drastic than X himself, and he had, particularly at that time, the ruthlessness of one who is newly, but wholly, detached from his own affections, and perhaps not sufficient tenderness for those who are not. I should moderate his advice if I were you (if you choose to accept it at all) and take the spirit rather than the letter of it. It is, of course, advice which any one of us could surely profit by, especially if we have a fair dose of heroism and a tremendous love of God. So far as heroism and the love of God goes, you have them both in that He's your real security, and the certainty that ultimately you will attain the heaven that *must begin* on earth....

17TH AUGUST, 1948

... I have been meaning to write to you, and wanting to do so very much ever since the letter you wrote to me before, saying that you were going to Walsingham; but I have really been simply exhausted by people and by the absurd *fight* and nervous exasperation that I have to endure for every single hour of work I do. The old wretched situation has arisen of having to work most of the night, because people take so much time by day, and of course never five minutes of real leisure—I am really so tired that I *know* I must put a stop to it, but then I've not got the energy to do so!

I think I will have to employ you as an occasional visiting confidential secretary to type answers to the countless lonely women who write from every part of the world. I am sure you would make a much better job of consoling them than I can!

I can't think what is in this room; I thought Jones [the cat] was snoring, but in spite of all wishful thinking to the contrary, I have been forced to admit that the sound of a cat snoring is coming from quite a different part of the room to the one where Jones is sleeping!

18TH AUGUST, 1948

In spite of the ghostly snoring cat, I fell asleep at this point and only woke, stiff as a dead cat myself, this morning, having lost what little time I had to write to you—and, with the day, a pile of wretched appointments and jobs to do against time.

23RD JANUARY, 1949

I was very sorry indeed to read so sad an account of you in your letter, and though I will…of course pray for you, and you have my deep sympathy, I really can't attempt to say *anything* that might (but more likely wouldn't) help—because, as you know, I know nothing whatever of the circumstances…you speak of.

If it is—what it might well be from the hints you give—a case of someone who is not free, then it may well be that it has been crippling and frustrating your life and actually holding the door shut to other people and experiences, without your realizing it. If so, now, although I know very well, and from experience, how such breaks or renunciations can hurt, and that, for good or ill, the hurt always remains with one—yet no sooner is such a decision really made than one finds those people and experiences that one has been denying, coming into one's life like shattering, unimaginable graces—not shattering in the destructive sense, but shattering the walls that any necessarily frustrating experience builds round us when we foster it.

Maybe, while you *feel* that you have shut the door on something which, if not exactly happiness, seemed better than it to you, you have in reality thrown it open to the true happiness which is really your ultimate good.

You are very wise to try to get a job; that is the very best practical course to take. I do hope something you can really bring a willing mind to will turn up for you.…

25TH MARCH, 1949

… I am very sorry you are so depressed, and I am afraid I can't say anything likely to help you. Regarding your "grand farewell"—as I really know nothing of the facts, I can't say much at all, excepting the probably feeble generalizations I have said or written already.

Here I can only pray for you. I know what it feels like to part from a man whom one is in love with, for I too have done so, years and years ago—and the years have not lessened or dimmed the love, even though he is dead now, shot in Russia by the Communists. I know what anguish such a parting can be, but tell you, in case you can find any ray of comfort for yourself in it, that certainly in my case it hasn't brought any sense of waste or frustration, but a kind of completeness and richness nothing else could have. I have never had any "feeling" of his nearness or anything since he died, but I *have* always *known* that he is alive and that one day, I devoutly hope, we shall meet. A few years of grief on earth are nothing compared to being together in eternity in God's presence. Also—and maybe this is more important—*because* I loved that man, I have loved many other people, animals and things. Perhaps later on you too will have these comforts.…

I am terribly sorry about Timmy [a cat]; pray for him to Blessed Martin de Porres, who just now is working a lot of miracles, and does them for animals as well as men. He cured a cat at death's door, the instant a relic (secondary) was put on him. I know what really awful misery it is to see one's animal suffer, and the frightful anxiety one feels for them. As you say, I miss Jones beyond words; he was nearly twenty years old, and it is as if part of myself has been torn out. I try to tell myself I owe it to the grand old boy not to let sadness wipe out the many beautiful and happy memories he gave to me.

You know, Christine, I come to agree more and more with *one* of the things X said about you—that you will never achieve peace until you put yourself blindly into the hands of someone else, whom you can trust, and allow them to decide for you, not only on big issues but in details of each day. If you had, for your writing and living, all the energy you put into indecision, there would be little you could not do! Why do you not go and have a talk with Fr. Y? He came here recently and I asked him if I could suggest it; he said, most certainly, and he is the most Christ-like and understanding human person—besides which he has got specialized knowledge of psychology and is a sort of fusion of priest, doctor and friend. I cannot imagine anyone more sure to understand and to be able to help you....

29TH APRIL, 1949

I am so very glad that you have seen—and like—Fr. X. I agree with you that he is a really holy man, and besides that, he has very deep understanding and insight. I only hope you will go on seeing him, as I *know* he has a real gift for psychological healing—just knowing him and seeing him, really *very* seldom, has done wonders for me myself.

Funny he offered you "Hope" as a working idea, because only about a week ago, as the result of a real act of contrition, I suddenly realized what hope is, and that I had *never* known before. I had always acted and reacted as if Faith could do everything, and all my sins just vanish in due course if I prayed and took practical steps to avoid the occasions of sin, and I was very discouraged to find that on the contrary they always got worse! Then, like a flash of light, I realized that *Hope* is a sort of splint on my broken spiritual limbs, which can keep me going and reasonably happy—also more humble—all the time; and it really has been my great support ever since.

I think you will only do yourself good by confiding in Fr. X. I should not worry about his sensitiveness; he is a real "other Christ," and what will give him real joy will be to be able to help you, and no one can help you really unless you are wholly frank with him. Never mind about showing ugly things; a real healer is like a doctor, who doesn't see a sore as ugly once he has put his balm on it, because he is only interested and concentrated on seeing the healing process on it. Remember…that it is at the sore place, and only there, that our healing begins; and that whenever healing does begin at a sore which you have had the courage and love to expose, there, in that sore spot, the healing of the whole world begins.…

St. Mark's Ward,
Westminster Hospital
23rd April, 1951

… I had the operation two weeks ago.… You will be astonished to hear that, much as I dreaded the public ward—and I *did* dread it, more than the operation—I have now learnt to be glad I am in it, and if I ever come again, which is all too likely, I will choose it! But I have a cubicle in it, which gives a lot of privacy, though the other patients, who are all very friendly, walk in and chat to me constantly; but anyhow I don't have to be perpetually exposed to the public gaze—and my admiration and liking for human nature has gone up by leaps and bounds since I came here. There is, no doubt, a communion with Christ through pain which gives people the power of *His* love, regardless of what, if anything, they believe.…

819 Nell Gwynn House
1st October, 1951

Thank you so very much for remembering my birthday, for writing to me, and for the lovely German angel Michael, whom I like very much, as he looks masculine and strong and not—like most English and French angels—daft. I shall put him in my Missal and say a prayer for you each time I see him there.

I did not know that your grandmother and B. had died; I do send you my deepest sympathy, and I know that however well prepared one is for the death of someone who is one's own flesh and blood, or an essential part of one's childhood, it always comes as a shock when it happens, and leaves one feeling that part of oneself has died with them.

I shall pray for them both, and with confidence that when the final reunion comes, you will find them in heaven, young and joyful and beautiful, coming to welcome you....

X

To a Young Friend Who Married and Settled Abroad

29TH OCTOBER, 1945

This *can* only be a very short little note to thank you for writing and to tell you what a tremendous comfort it is to me to know that my books find a response in you—that they mean something to you. You are incredibly generous, but what you say is a real source of strength to me and gives me heart to go on, and I just want you to know that I am grateful to you for taking the trouble to write.

22ND OCTOBER, 1945

… I wanted to say that I can perfectly understand the sense of fear you have about prayer, for I have had it too, but I think that a simple desire that God should act in you as He wills is sufficient; I do not think it need even be formulated in words. If you just say something (or mean something without saying it) like "I am afraid, but I don't want to be; I don't feel as if I trust you, but I do," God will do the rest, and I think He will enter into your night, as the ray of the sun enters into the dark, hard earth, driving right down to the roots of the tree, and there, unseen, unknown, unfelt in the darkness, filling the tree with life, a sap of fire that will suddenly break out, high above that darkness, into living leaf and flower.

"Praying by proxy" is a good expression, and I don't think it would be a thing to deny oneself, because first of all just imagine the *immense* relief you could give to me simply by not resisting any kind of prayer or movement towards God or man that my poor stammering rhythms could help you to: then—and this is so much more important—the whole meaning of the Mystical Body, Christ on earth, is that we *are* all "good with others' goodness" and guilty with others' guilt, praying with others' prayers, and so on. A soldier was talking to me the other day about a long route march he had made between two prison camps; he said something which seemed to me to be the most wonderful unconscious description of the Mystical Body, from the other angle, the angle of the Passion: "After we had been marching a long time, I didn't *feel myself* aching any more, I felt the tiredness of the chap behind me aching in my bones."

I think that's happened to you in a very big way and that you, thinking yourself frustrated from a part in the world's suffering, have ceased feeling yourself aching in you, because all the world is crowned with thorns in your mind; but then you should surely allow the prayer and joy and goodness of others also to come in—for otherwise it is "No" to Christ in them and a kind of thwarting of their love.

I fear I am being very confused.

My own feeling is that I must always look at God; I would not dare to form an ideal for myself and try to reach it, or to get a good realization of my sinfulness and dwell on it. Contrition, for my weak nature, must mean looking up and seeing how forgiving, and how *joyfully* forgiving, God is: adoration only, so to speak, turning in His direction.

I am confident not only that the great stream of light and love that is pent up in you *can* come out, but that it is going to.

As to my rhythms, I can only feel, as I presume a mother would over her children, that their failures are very obvious to me but I must forgive them; and what could console me is if, in spite of being what they are, they can do something in this world for others. Don't think they aren't for you, they are indeed for you, they are yours; think of them as yours. You are so kind to them, too....

25TH OCTOBER, 1945

… I've not only read your last letter once, but many times, and it reassures me that this darkness you experience is part of the necessary darkness for growth; I mean the seed of the word of God *must* grow secretly in darkness. I will answer all you say in person, and please *don't* hesitate to write; I want you to, only I am a very *unsatisfactory* answerer, owing, not to disinclination, but to too little time; so people who are near enough to be seen do get miserable letters from me—what Frank Sheed calls "wretched little puppies of letters."

When you have gone to Portugal I will write you grown-up dogs at least!

I don't think you will find our contact fades when you have gone; it may be stronger, and I am sure that in doing your job you will find great strength, besides there being, in spite of much irreligion, a very deep undercurrent of real faith in Portugal.…

28TH OCTOBER, 1945

… In the meantime, the only thing that I can see that will help you is to learn to love yourself, to forgive yourself, to be kind to yourself, by looking outwards to God, by accepting the fact that you are infinitely loved by Infinite Love, and that if you will only cease to build up notions of the perfection you demand of yourself, and lay your soul open to that love, you will cease to fear, and you will cease to be exhausted as soon as you stop fighting one part of yourself with another. I can only pray for you and beg you to turn your face to this immense love and power and cast all your fear on to it. You should try to realize that in you is the power, strength and love of Christ, that you can carry all that darkness and not go under, if you realize that it isn't you but He who will carry it; also, if you will try to realize that in you Christ lives His risen life, that He has already *overcome death*—died and risen from death and overcome it; that it is the *Risen Christ*, who has already defeated death, who lives in you. If you will only realize that, you will soon be convinced that you will also come right up through the darkness into the light. One can't think of God at all without thinking of *light*; at least I can't.... Try to believe that life is in you like a seed, pushing, striving, struggling up to light. Instead of fighting yourself, let this seed of supernatural life fight its way out through darkness, just as an ordinary seed fights up through the darkness and heaviness of the hard, frozen earth. First it has to sharpen its own green blade in the night and cut through the ground, or pierce the wood if it is a leaf on the tree, but suddenly it breaks into flower or leaf; and when it does that, it does not see its own beauty—the world outside it sees that; what it sees is the glorious sun that drew it up out of the darkness. Light. So too will it be with you; your soul, your mind will break into flower and you will find it is flowering in the midst of light, the light of Truth and Beauty and Life.

I enclose a good translation of the *Veni, Sancte Spiritus*. Try to say it—read it—will it.

God bless you.

I'm sorry I can't write a decent letter, but I am snowed under with people and work.

My love, and have no fear, for all will be well.

4TH NOVEMBER, 1945

Thank you very much indeed for sending me the rhythms. I have so far only had a chance to read them once, and the once has impressed me with their wonderful *realness* and—though you probably will dispute this—sincerity, and I do think it would be tremendously worth while if you went on trying to express yourself that way, or, as you grow in awareness of God's beauty all around you and, though unperceived by you, within you, trying to express *that* beauty. It may not be your first vocation to write poetry, but it is certainly part of you, and would be at least a step—if not a great flight—in the direction of your vocation....

I don't know what you mean by saying you were "rather beastly." You have never been that, or anything like it, at least not here. I may be very tiresome in this, but the fact is, I see the person God loves in you, not the person you hate, and I assure you I don't want you to run down this dear and lovable person, whom God loves.

Yes, what you said in another letter is true. You don't belong to yourself, and you must be kind to the person who belongs to God.

I can't write a proper letter; I have an accumulation of things to get through. But you are all the time in my prayers—all the time—and also I pray to your guardian angel to look after you, which he does of course, but to open your mind to the Light. I am sure this angel, whose whole marvellous existence is concentrated, at God's command, on you alone, must see you as utterly lovely, because the object of God's absolute love.…

7TH NOVEMBER, 1945

… I enclose an unpublished rhythm which perhaps has some elements of your experience in it.

THE CONVERT
(1)
… Then, Lord—
Inevitable Love!—
if it must be,
purify me!
Heat of the Sun,
drive down
to the roots of me;
down
down
down
to the dark roots

of the tree,
Sap of molten fire.
The earth is still cold and hard.
When the earth is warm
from the sun I do not see,
life will be conscious of love.
In the dark
and the cold,
I believe
in the green leaf.
In the frost
and the hard crust,
I hope
in the flower.
In the cold winter,
unloving,
I love.

(2)
… Then, Lord,
Inevitable Love,
if it must be, live in me!
I am driven through
with your life,
cut open by spears of it
like dark earth,
hard earth,
parched earth;
cut open
with sharp
and delicate
green blades.
… Then, Lord,
Inevitable Love,

if it must be,
flower in me.
I am broken open
with bursting buds;
since I abandoned nothingness
to Love
I am broken open
with the bursting of buds.
I must reach upwards
because of the rising sap,
because of the molten fire
in the sleeping roots.

(3)
I must reach up,
and up
and up,
and the darkness
at the root
be in the core
of the sweet,
and bright,
potential fruit
on the bough.
Lord, Lord, Lord,
Inevitable Love,
since it must *be,*
purify me!

26TH NOVEMBER, 1945

Your letter has come and it is such real joy to me—above all to see that Portugal looks like being the right place for you, anyhow for some time.

I thought it would be, and your letter adds to my hope that I thought truly....

I do hope you will write often and freely and without hesitation or worries. Don't ever think "Oh, I wish I had not put that," or, "I'm sure I did not make such-and-such clear" and so on: just be at ease; where I am concerned you need not have any anxieties....

Now then, do not, I beg you, worry about living an extroverted life there, or imagine pride in the idea of flying to God in everyone you meet and come into contact with. If you allow yourself to decide that there is pride in this idea, you then will really jump right into it, because it is not your idea or my idea, but Christ's idea, which He has so clearly stated—"If you do it to the least of these little ones, you do it to me."

I feel convinced that all this outgoing—the posters you are making (which sound glorious!), the laughter, the dancing, everything you do with everyone, is a real fling of the heart to God every time, and the truest prayer. Moreover, I am sure that the kindness of those great-hearted people is *His* invitation to you to know Him better and love Him more, in and through them. For heaven's sake, dearest, do not let morbid turning inwards drag back your mind and heart from Christ in His people, to yourself, but if you sometimes do do that because you can't help it, lift yourself up at once, and forget it; as soon as the mood lifts, *run* back to Him, *jump* up to Him, and laugh with Him—you can.

I want you to realize that I am your friend. I have not got much power or strength or anything to give of soul or body, but *what* I have, I do and shall give, and you must always feel that you have at least one friend in England, who is deeply concerned with everything that concerns you.

I saw two cripples in Brompton Road years ago, both a bit helpless, but getting along quite well by leaning on one another. I thought then: "There goes poor human nature! When we try to stand alone in our poor twisted weak state we are bound to come a cropper, but when our very infirmity makes us humbly loving to one another and we lean on each other for mutual support, then we can get along and even get home!" I have never forgotten that moving couple; strange, isn't it, how from someone that we pass once in the street we can learn something that remains with us for strength or comfort all our life long? …

You know, you have no occasion to be grateful to me, but I have occasion to be grateful to you, and indeed I am; a thousand times a day some second of gratitude goes to you. You have revealed many beautiful things to me, and vast realms of thought; you have released deep and good affections in me, and you have shown me some aspects of Christ's Passion of which you are probably not aware, even on the physical plane—which I am very far indeed from despising in a life which is, as ours is, sacramental. You have given me such a lot—for example, your warm coat and dress, and when I put it on, it is a pleasure to think that this warmth is so truly willed to me by your kindness. It reminds me of Jonathan taking off his robe and putting it on David—a story which always moves me so deeply because I see in it a most touching symbol of Christ putting *His* warm, loving humanity on to us like a garment.

Then your bicycle—I did not even thank you for it, but I just do not know what to say. I'm not used to such generosity, but how I really do feel grateful at your being willing to give it when your father had made it for you—and it will be such a real blessing in Iris's country cottage… which is four miles from the church… I shall feel you are carrying me to God! …

819 Nell Gwynn House
2nd June, 1946

… You will see that I have a different flat, 819—still in the same house, but on the eighth floor, and it is wonderful, full of air and light, and bells and wings. Birds seem to fly round the windows all the time and I am simply encircled by the Blessed Sacrament. There are windows all round (it is a corner flat) and one side looks out to the Oratory, the other to St. Mary's, Cadogan Street, and Westminster Cathedral; so far as the other flats are concerned it is silent. One does not even hear their wireless in here, but I wake to the sound of the first Angelus from the

Caryll Houselander

Oratory and hear all the Sanctus and Benediction bells all day—and to have this lovely light always—light at night as well as by day—moonlight, which I had almost forgotten....

During the last two months life has been really very difficult as X was suddenly taken ill. It was agony to stand by helpless to help, and watch, and in a very humble way and from a very great distance I realized how all real contemplation of the Passion began on Calvary in Our Lady when, as the Gospel puts it, "There stood by the cross of Jesus, Mary His mother." Just to look—to be unable to comfort or ease, but to be there and look. Do you know, I feel sure that such contemplation, being helpless but *aware* of Christ suffering in humanity, is demanded of our generation. It is a true contemplation, for it involves sharing, suffering what one sees with eyes of the body or of the intellect or of the soul, in oneself.

So long as one can do *anything* to alleviate—such as the First Aid, etc., one gave in the war—this very doing and giving of something else saves us to a certain extent from giving *self*; but as soon as one is helpless and can do nothing—except *be there* in the presence of one whom one loves and who is in complete pain—then one knows what real contemplation means. I think the contemplation asked of our generation (and I am certain you personally have this vocation, which is why I am labouring this point to you!) goes through certain clearly defined stages, just as the cloistered variety of contemplation does.

First one has to learn to see and to love Christ in man, in one another, and this can only be done by the practice of simple human love; and then one has to learn (in an age of fun and wasted activity) that one can do nothing; and then one gets caught up into the universal suffering, and the real knowledge of Christ and His Passion begins. But I find, now that I have written this, it does not in the least express what I mean now. Now perhaps I ought to destroy this letter, in case it gives a wrong impression? But if I do it may be ages before I get time to write again, so I won't. I'll leave it and hope that you may get out of it some meaning *better* than the one I cannot clarify! ...

X is now marvellously better and I can resume my normal life and am trying to make up for lost time—not that time is ever really lost; it is merely that sometimes it is used as God plans instead of as we do, and we consider it to be *lost*! ...

10TH SEPTEMBER, 1946

... You say, "Will I ever be able to become good and sincere and true to God?" My belief is that you *are*, and you need only to trust Him completely; then one day you will realize this suddenly, when you least expect it, in the form of peace.

But say the *memorare* often—the result of it is *wonderful*, as I have learnt lately. I seldom say prayers by heart, or *say* much at all, but I was persuaded to say this prayer by a convert Jew, so to please him I did, and have found the answers to it astonishing. Some people think it foolish to ask God for little things, but I do not think it matters at all what one asks for, so long as in asking for *anything* one recognizes one's own dependence on God, His Fatherhood and His longing to give *Himself*, no matter in what way. Sometimes a tiny childish thing brings home to us more than a big thing the *intense love* which can make Omnipotence concerned, for our sakes, with trifles.

Tell me, please, much more about yourself, your mind, your work, your daily life, your friends. I want to be able to picture you and what you are doing all day. Spain sounds so extraordinarily interesting too. But it is not just Spain, but you in Spain, that I want to know about.

I have been revising *This War Is the Passion*† for which there is still a demand.... I have put in eight new articles and cut a few out, etc. The new ones are mainly about reparation, a technique for fear, the Mass and so on, and one about Our Lady's mind. Many English Catholics like to think that Our Lady had no mind, but this is a view I do not share!

---

† Re-issued as *The Comforting of Christ*.

Now I am finishing what I call my "novel" [*The Dry Wood*], but it is not the least bit a novel; it is really a spiritual book in the form of fiction, or rather simply a book about life, but the supernatural as well as the natural life. Its theme is the suffering of children, and I thought I had chosen a simple little story within my scope to handle. I was wrong; it is an immense theme, and seems to include the universe, and is vastly beyond my range or power—yet I am bound to finish it, as much as one is bound to give birth to a child, even if it is stillborn. But I beg you, pray hard for this poor book; you can understand as few can the dark, blank anguish which has held me up and paralyzed the writing of it again and again....

Do you still write some rhythms? I feel sure that by that means you lay firmer and firmer hold on realities. Anyone who can hear and know the essential rhythm in all things must do so, and this you certainly can and do....

6TH OCTOBER, 1946

Thank you for your kind and lovely letter—you are always so tolerant and patient with me, and I always keep you waiting so long.

This is only a brief answer to yours, in order *not* to keep you waiting, especially as you ask me for some definite advice. About the... Convent—it is clear to me that I would be presumptuous in saying Yes or No, as this is a decision which you alone can make; but what I do feel, after thinking and praying very much about it, is this: that if you do enter, it should only be with the fullest intention of complete obedience, and no reservations at all: that you would eat as the others do, and would write if told to, and would take it on faith that your life, since you undertook it for love of God, is pleasing to Him. Any other attitude would, I feel certain, end in leaving the convent after a short while. You alone can know if that spirit is possible.

I am sorry to seem so vague about the convent, but this is so obviously something that you and God can decide, and no one else.

9TH MARCH, 1947

Thank you very much for your letter of February 2nd, which I meant to answer at once—and did not—alas! I am intensely interested to hear that you have become engaged to a Spanish doctor. I hope and pray that it will result in a happy marriage, and I would like to hear more about it—and him! Not from motives of curiosity, believe me, but because anything which affects your life and happiness interests me profoundly. Quite frankly, I was pleased that you had not entered the convent. Personally I think a religious vocation is something about which one cannot be in doubt and indecision, excepting perhaps for a very short time. I think it has an inescapable, compelling quality, and I would always tend to take hesitation concerning whether one has it or not as a sign that one has not! However, I may be entirely wrong, as I have not got one myself and never have had, so have nothing to go on but other people's experience and my own imagination; and moreover there are always unusual and exceptional cases, whatever the rule....

I wonder what the conditions in Spain are like. I have never known anything like the sadness here, and the inward tragedy. In spite of spates of articles and speeches on spiritual revivals, spiritual leadership and so on, the majority seem to be without faith, without any integrating purpose, without an ideal and without hope—and, though few realize it, in another three or four months we have a fair chance of being without food!—or anyhow with a real minimum. Only one answer to it—to try to go on loving; every act, every word, every thought of love has immense value, and I am sure that nothing else has any. Please pray for me and get the strength of spirit for me which I lack, and know well that I lack....

God keep you: may He shine on your mind and set your feet in the way.

Caryll Houselander

4TH AUGUST, 1948

… Strange to relate, between Christmas and Easter I was (with Iris) looking after a baby.… I never before knew what an infant teaches about God, and how surrender to it, is surrender to Him—and when that surrender is made, there is something *more* than peace in one's life, something which does not preclude suffering, but makes it bearable.

Do say—or, if you can't say it, hold on to—your rosary. Just hold it in your hand; it is a great power.

4TH MARCH, 1949

I have just received the joyful news that you have a little girl. I am overjoyed and full of gratitude about it, and rejoiced too to read in the telegram which X has kindly sent to me, that you are both very happy.

Please thank X for the telegram and congratulate him for me.

I am simply longing to hear everything about the little girl, and everything you will tell me about your own reactions to her. I feel sure that they are full of joy and peace, and that this little girl has come as a wonderful blessing to you, who will bring only happiness into your life and X's life and into the world.

I want to know the serious things about her, but the so-called superficial ones too, for I always attach significance to names, dates, hours and things like that.

When was she born—what date, and on what Feast? I actually got your wire on the day after Ash Wednesday; was she born on Ash Wednesday? She seems set for sanctity, if so! Or it may have been on Shrove Tuesday, and she is set for pancakes and fun and all the jolly things you don't do in Lent! At what hour was she born? What does she weigh? What is her name to be? On what date will she be baptized? What colour is her hair? Her eyes? I know she was born with blue eyes, but is their tendency to grey or brown or green or black or more blue? What skin has she—golden, white, pink, brown? And—oh, this is *very* interesting to me—exactly what shape are her hands? Are they long, tapering, or round or square fingers?

Now please write and answer every one of these questions, so that, though the sea is between us, I can *know* and see your baby a little, and when I have the delight of really seeing her, she will not be a stranger to me. She will *not* be, because I shall pray for her a lot, and in that mysterious country of prayer I shall get to know her even before we meet.

I am very happy for you both, for I know that there is nothing in this world so wonderful as to have a child; it is truly the presence of God in your home, even in your arms.

My love to all three of you, and may God keep you all and bless you more and more, and give you the grace of knowing and realizing every moment of your blessedness.

25TH JULY, 1949

… I just want to return your *lovely* photographs and to assure you that every word you tell me about this little Christ-Child is of *absorbing* interest to me, from so far. I love her.…

30TH NOVEMBER, 1949

… Your visit was much too short. I so want to talk to you, and would have given worlds to get you to myself for a time and to hear about *yourself*. But still, the thing that matters *most* of all was to see M., and that is accomplished. I *really* do not know how to express the effect she had on me; she is the loveliest and literally the most *heavenly* baby I have ever seen—in every way she seemed like a little Infant Christ. How I do wish we lived nearer together; I should like to come and help you by some really humble service for *her*, like washing and cleaning, and to be often in her radiant and purifying presence.

Certainly…you are a *wonderful* mother. How you keep her so clean and dainty and beautifully dressed, and how you have fostered and saved that tiny, but, I think, strong burning flame of life in her, is really a kind of miracle of human love. You seem to me to have redeemed countless women who fail in motherhood, and I am quite sure that your love for darling little M. is radiating outwards in huge circles of light, which in a mysterious way are bringing grace and love to many, many children all over the world.

Now about Clare's dress.… I think it is perfect, and the work on it is amazing. I love its bright flowers, and so does Clare. She was very delighted with herself and stood looking at herself in the glass, stroking the dress and saying "Pitty." Then she fetched her brush and stood to have her hair brushed and fluffed out, and demanded to have her blue shoes on! She certainly realized that every detail must be perfect for her dress.

She is coming to stay for a few days next week and having a little birthday party; two small boys are coming, and she will wear her dress and cut her cake—in it, she will look like a bride.

Now, when I left you that day in Battersea, I did not go to the bus at all; I turned into Battersea Park and walked through it all the way. I felt that I could not go straight from the loveliness of M. to the grey sordidness of every day. The trees and the sky and the water in the park softened the return from heaven to earth.…

Before I forget—I am sending a little cross to M. for Christmas, but I don't know if you will let her wear it; if not, give it to some other little child. It is made of pottery, which sounds very odd, but is not so odd as it sounds. It is made of *tiny* pottery flowers, forget-me-nots, but with one little pink rose in the middle. It is because of the pink rose that you may not like to put on M., who must wear blue and white. It was made by hand by a person who lives near the church[†] I spoke of, and who was selling some of her work in aid of the church. The people constantly give the priest money to heat and repair the church, but he just gives it all away to the poor, which delights me!

---

† In Prince's Risborough, Buckinghamshire.

After Christmas, when I hope to be less busy than now, I will make M. a little soft doll. Not because she hasn't got better ones than I can make—I am sure she has—but because children seem to like home-made toys, and I should certainly like making it for her.…

26TH OCTOBER, 1953

What a great joy to receive your letter, and what a great honour, and joy too, to be made godmother to your little girl, A. Thank you very much indeed for that.

Certainly you may rest assured that I will pray for her every day—and I feel so overjoyed about her that, if you can't possibly come and visit me during the next few years, I will try to overcome my neurosis about going away from home and visit you! I will also do my best to be a good godmother about birthdays and will write to her! …

I am sure that, brought up with all the great love and intelligence that you and X will pour out on her, not to mention her sister and little brothers, she will grow up a very lovely person. Being sensitive—even "over-sensitive"—is really an advantage, rather than a disadvantage, in this sad world. At least, I think so.

Lately I have thought a lot about the wonderful mystery of individuality—I mean, that God has chosen from all eternity to create each individual born into this world. Not one comes by accident—each one in His decree is intended to be *one with Him* for ever in eternity: to be "another Christ" on this earth.…

XI

To Mrs. Boardman

Caryll had never met Mrs. Boardman before receiving a letter from her asking for her help. This often came about through Caryll's books, but this acquaintance by post grew into a most close relationship. In some ways it is the most interesting of all Caryll's correspondences. Lasting from 1946 until the year of her death, it shows the events of both their lives woven into a significant pattern. As time went on Mrs. Boardman's daughters were received into the Church, and the elder especially grew close to Caryll and was as interested as her mother in Iris's granddaughter. Little Clare was also Caryll's pride and joy and on her she lavished the love which would have gone to a child of her own. To Clare we owe one of her books, The Passion of the Infant Christ.

11TH OCTOBER, 1946

Thank you very much for your letter. I am more than glad that you have written to me, and I am most deeply sympathetic with you in the really great trial and suffering that you are undergoing.

I do realize it all, and can imagine the intensity of feeling against Catholicism that you are surrounded with, for I have known it very often and met it also in people very dear to me, as well as in the friends and relations of very many converts. Indeed, nearly all converts have to suffer it—a fact which does not make it any easier for any individual one, unless it is any help to realize that one is not alone. Perhaps that is a help—particularly when (and this I can assure you is so) many who have been at the point at which you are now, and have thought, as you think, that the next step can hardly be endured, and who did go on, found that God came much more than halfway to meet them, and many seemingly hopeless obstacles vanished, so that now, though not free from trials and suffering, they have attained wonderful peace and abundant grace to suffer the price of it; and in many cases the cost has been far less than they ever dared to hope.

You ask how I see your problem. Does Our Lord really demand of you that you come into the Church, even though you know it will cause great suffering to those you love? Yes: I am quite convinced that if you really believe that the Roman Catholic Church *is* the Church He founded, He does ask this of you.

You ask what right have you to "torment these people, for the sake of spiritual convictions, spiritual 'security'?"

The answer, as I see it, is: First of all, this is a matter between yourself and God. If you believe in God, then you are bound to believe that He wishes you to "save your soul"—which means, to be united to Him, to fulfil the purpose for which He made you. Each individual is responsible for his own soul, not for the sake of spiritual convictions and security, but for the sake of God's will, for the sake of responding to His love, and accepting *His life*. If you have seen that His truth is in this or that Church, then it is not even a choice; it is a matter of salvation to accept His truth. Our Lord has Himself answered about people: He *says* that He brings not peace but a sword, that He will set people dear to one another and in one family at variance, that anyone who does not put Him before father and mother and all who are dear, cannot follow Him.

There is no way out. Think, if you elect to compromise, nothing anyone says to you can give you inward peace—your own heart will torment you. If I wrote and said: "God will understand; go on with a false conscience," would that get down to the depth of your soul and give it rest?

No, of course it *could* not. The way is clear and unmistakable, and I have no doubt it is the way, and the only way, to peace and happiness for you.

Now, I know how hard all that sounds, and I know, too, that if it just depended upon your will it would be too hard; but there are many considerations which, if you have patience to listen to them, will show you that it will not be so terrible as it seems.

Before speaking of the solid support and help you will have from God, I want to say something about your family. The suffering that they will have is, I can't help thinking, of their own making, and will be less intense—and certainly less lasting—than you think. You are doing them no injury; on the contrary, you are doing them a service. To start with, on the purely natural plane, if you deny yourself what you now know to be the real source of life and grace, you will gradually become warped, unhappy and empty; you will not really be able to help your children, for there will be no fountain of life in yourself to do so. So far, therefore, as their faith in their own religion depends on, or is stimulated by, your influence, it will—after a few years or sooner—suffer far more terribly than by your becoming a Catholic; for they, if they do not realize that you do not *believe* in Anglo-Catholicism, will sense the fact at all events [that] it has given you no inward joy, that it has failed you; they will indeed be children asking for bread and receiving a stone, because in deep matters like this you cannot deceive.

If you become a Catholic, however much you are misunderstood or persecuted, the fountain of life, Christ Himself, will be in you. Your children will sense that; when they look to you for help they will find it, and this will increase their faith in Christ, whatever their personal way to Him may be. In any case, sooner or later they would realize that you had not followed your own conviction, and this is a cruelly bad example, far more really wronging them than allowing them to feel a little distress (which will pass) because of misconception and prejudice. Also, from the point of view of your husband, if you attain to peace of conscience, clearly you will be an increasingly rich and balanced and loving human being; otherwise, spiritual frustration will lead to human frustration, incompleteness, perhaps bitterness, and he will be the sufferer.

But there is a far more important supernatural element. You are being invited to become in very truth "another Christ," to enter fully into His life through the sacraments. He is offering you, holding out to you, His own heart to love with, His own power to save the world; He asks you to exchange your weak, trembling heart for His strong, loving heart. You are among those who are chosen to share His suffering and His joy, to be a redeemer in the world through your union with Him, which gives your every simplest action His power with God the Father.

In a word, Christ offers you the power of His prayers, His love to give to your family, your friends, and to the whole world, His hands to heal the world's grief, His love to save it. With this power, you can win for your own family all the graces that will bring them, each in their own way, into the closest union with God possible to each one of them.

At this moment the world, the whole human race, does so need "other Christs" who alone can atone for its sins and bring peace into it.

The experience of many converts whose environment seemed as hopeless, even more hopeless, than yours, has been invariably that once they had told their people definitely—or at all events, once they had *done* it—the fury abated. Ultimately, if you use great charity and patience, they are usually converted themselves.

Now I am sure that once you are inside the Church and able to receive the sacraments, you will find that the suffering asked of you is far more tolerable than you could ever have imagined. For so long as you have received "sacraments" in good faith in the Anglican Church, you have most surely received Christ's grace through them, just as your children are doing now; but the difference between this and the reality is something which can only be known when it is experienced. Not, indeed, because of any emotional feeling at the time of receiving the sacrament, but because of the courage, peace and strength that grow almost unperceived in the soul, and the very slowly assimilated realization of the power and presence of Christ in you. Things which seem impossible without the sacraments become even easy with them.

To come to a practical matter: I would advise you to make up your mind, to surrender your will to God, and to tell *Him* you will; then, having made your offering, spend some days in prayer to obtain the courage and grace to go on. You have prayed and have not yet, as you think, had the complete answer. This is usually because you have not given Our Lord something He asks for, in order to answer you. For example, when He worked miracles He asked for some trifle which one would suppose useless—as, for example, the loaves and fishes for the feeding of five thousand; and again, for the Mass, He asks the offering of the simple substance of bread and wine for the miracle of the Consecration. You say, "He hasn't worked the miracle," "He hasn't given me the courage I need." Well, the answer usually is: "You have not given Him anything to work the miracle with." Of course, He *can* do some miracles without, but usually He asks us to give something, and, if the miracle you ask is personal transubstantiation—that *you* may be changed into Him—then clearly, unless you offer *yourself*—all of yourself—He can't do it, for what has He got to change?

God is *never* outdone in generosity. If your self-offering is sincere, and is made, no matter how you tremble in making it, He will then give you the grace you need.

It is well, after making your self-offering, to pray very much to Our Lady, and you know she has been through all this, and she is a great example of how to act with those you love. Recall the bitter misunderstanding of St. Joseph when she had first conceived the Infant Christ: *she* had to give pain to one whom she loved, and she did not try to explain to him. As a rule, argument does not help, and it is better to imitate her and wait for God to enlighten others. After having offered yourself to God, surrendered to Him and prayed to Our Lady, then only, if I were you, would I go to a priest and commence instruction.

I do not know any priests in that part of the world, but could find out about them from Mr. Sheed, who seems to know all the priests in England!—unless you feel better able to find out yourself.

Naturally you know best how to deal with your own children, and how they can best accept things, so I am even more tentative over this than the rest, but I would advise frankness from the start. I should explain to them that through your prayer and the graces God has given to you *through* the Anglican Church, you have come to believe in the Catholic Church; that the Anglican Church, though, in the mind of the Catholic Church, not part or branch of the Catholic Church, contains many millions of souls who are far more truly one with the Catholics because they, through their good faith, their love of God and their true Christian baptism, belong to the spirit of the Church. Very far from separating yourself from your children, you are drawing closer to them, but you do not ask or expect them to understand that yet. That you are not making any attempt to persuade *them* to change: they have the use of reason and are bound, as you are too, to follow their own conscience in the light they have. You and they must agree in this—that each must be loyal to truth *as she sees it*: and you will all be together in the degree of your love of Christ.

I think you should go to your child's confirmation, and in every way help and encourage them in their practice of religion.

Now would you like me to put you into touch with other converts who would understand your difficulties and with whom you could correspond? I know one who is very wonderful and, like you, has "arrived" through years of reading. She…has a grown-up son and daughter, a charming husband who is *bitterly* anti-Catholic; she is very human *and very* humourous, has gone through agony to come into the Church, and is quite alone in it.

… There is no detail of what you have to go through that she would not understand.

If this letter seems to you hard, conceited, bossy and interfering, please forgive me. The fact is, I am at present overwhelmed with work of several kinds and have terribly little time for writing letters, and so I have to be as brief as I can, and this does not allow me to soften things down and explain as often as I should that I am only offering an opinion, without authority—and so on.

I will (and have) pray for you, and if I can do anything more to help I shall be very glad to do it.

20TH OCTOBER, 1946

Thank you for your letter. You certainly have acted generously to God now, and I feel certain He will give you grace that you haven't yet imagined, to go on and endure the necessary suffering. I do feel very deeply for you, *both* with regard to the whole thing, the misunderstanding of those you love, *and* the terribly aggravating details and added trials which you mention in this letter....

Now we come to the most vital point of all. I fully agree with you that the time in which you may no longer receive Communion in the Anglican Church or in the Catholic Church is appallingly hard, but it does *not* mean that you are cut off from the sacraments or the grace of them, even though it may feel as if it does. It is a time, as you truly say, during which you need God's help as never before, but you can and will have it.

The sacraments received in the Anglican Church conveyed God's grace to you, because of your faith and your desire to receive Our Lord. You were making spiritual Communions when you received Holy Communion, and the grace you had came to you direct from the Blessed Sacrament. Now, if you will make regular spiritual Communions, at home, in your garden, or, if you can do this, at Mass in the Catholic church, you will receive Our Lord through them.

If you stop praying between the two Churches, so to speak, then indeed you will flounder, and the bewildering temptation to do so is very real. I know, alas, many who have fallen into it.

Of course you do already belong to the Catholic Church; of that there is no doubt. In a way you always have, but now it should be in a much more conscious way. The way you will be able to keep your place on your battle-ground will be by doing everything human and concrete that you can to help yourself to realize that you are wholly and utterly one with all Catholics living and dead; that you are now as much a Catholic as I am, or the priest, or any Catholic, from the Pope to the last baptized baby in Nigeria! You are now surrendered to God and are doing all in your power to complete it. You must think of all the angels surrounding you, all the saints and all the souls in Purgatory interceding for you; and of all the Catholics, even all Nature, in turn looking *to* you to be its voice, to pray for it.

If you can, you will find it a great help to go to Mass, making your spiritual Communion there; and as you will soon be obliged to start going to Mass in the Catholic church, I think you might as well (from the family point of view) start now. Alas, this going to Mass, when it starts, is almost invariably the signal for a fresh outburst of feeling, and this increases your troubles at a moment when above all you want as much inward peace as you can get. As there is always trouble at the time when you announce your intention of becoming a Catholic, if you start going to Mass at the same time, the one bout of anger covers that too!—rather like when a convicted burglar owns up to a dozen or so other burglaries, in order that the one sentence may cover them all! …

19TH NOVEMBER, 1946

… I am so sorry about the delay in your instruction, but unquestionably it could only have happened for God's purpose, and I am very convinced that quite suddenly the whole situation will be clarified and then you may (and may not!) see what His purpose is.

After all, this is a kind of very intimate birth of Christ in your own life, and if you consider how every plan of Our Lady's was upset at Christ's actual birth, every dream of St. Joseph's overthrown, and what, if one may say it reverently, an absolute muddle seemed to be in progress, humanly speaking—and then, how suddenly it all shone out, as clear and simple as the star of Bethlehem! Well, you can see that Our Lady and St. Joseph are the people to ask for help, and you will get it.…

Caryll Houselander

About the books. One prayerbook I would advise would also answer (partly) your question about the Missal. This book is a very simple, very lovely book of prayers called *Mysteries of the Mass in Reasoned Prayers*, and is by Father William Roche, S.J.... These prayers are meant to be Mass prayers, and they are a most lucid and beautiful instruction on the Mass too. I think the writer really intended them to be used more as meditation outside of the Mass, to make it easier for one to follow the Mass without any book at all. Incidentally, to help one to weave the sacrifice of the Mass into and all through one's daily life and to relate everything to it, it is invaluable.

Personally, I divide my Mass broadly into sorrow for sin, offering of self, adoration and communion with Christ and all men, and *say* what I like: when I get *particularly* wandering and distracted, I do read the Missal, but only regular prayers. I try to read through the others overnight, the night before, and to make the Introit, the little opening prayer that gives the character of the Mass of the day (i.e. joyful, penitential, etc.), the keynote of my whole day. I would strongly advise you to get Father Martindale's book, *The Mind of the Missal*—a magnificent explanation: also his two C.T.S. pamphlets—one is, I think, called just *At Mass* or *The Mass*, the other, *What Is He Doing at the Altar?*—both *very* valuable.

... If you have not read it, I would get *The Virtues of the Divine Child* by Daniel Considine, S.J., and everything else you can get by him: likewise all the books of Father R.H.J. Steuart, S.J.

... I heard today of an entire family whom I knew some years ago all being converted. The son asked prayers years ago for "something to happen" to make it easy for him to break the news of his intended conversion to his family, all extremely bigoted against Catholics. We—that is, friends, of whom I was one—prayed, of course, but nothing happened and he lost courage and did not go on. Today I have a letter from his mother, after at least ten years' silence, saying that suddenly, inexplicably, the entire family were converted, and amazed to discover that the son had for all these years carried a heavy heart because he lacked the courage of his faith! Certainly the prayers *were* answered. They have, all twelve of them, been received!

22ND JANUARY, 1947

… I am very sympathetic with you indeed and know how very lonely you must feel; and I know too that the greatest of all possible human sufferings is the misunderstanding and antagonism of those one loves. It is rather aggravated, I fear, by the attitude of priests and other holy persons from whom one asks for comfort. This is, I think, because, as is only natural, there are few indeed who, having arrived at a really deep sense of the reality of divine things, the inner meaning of suffering and the wonder of the joy just round the corner, still realize *wholly* the misery one feels when one is far off still from such *realization*, however much one believes in it. They are so profoundly conscious of the hidden good for us that they do not always remember what it *feels* like at the stage when, though we hang on like grim death to the good, it doesn't seem worth it. We have to take the advice of priests as we take the advice of doctors when they recommend drastic and painful treatment, knowing it is the painful way followed by happy life, or compromise followed by death.

But whom, then, *can* we go to for comfort?—because we need comfort, sympathy, love, as well as wisdom and practical help and cure; in fact, we not only need help, but that someone should be as concentrated on us as we are on ourselves, supporting us, loving us, feeling deeply for us, every second of the day and night. Well, Our Lord is the only one who can answer that need. If you go often to visit the Blessed Sacrament, and pray in the presence of the Blessed Sacrament, tell Our Lord in your own words, or your own tears, or your own dumbness, that you can hardly suffer it. Ask Him to help; you can be perfectly certain that He will.

Our Lady understands, too; she went through just this experience, and if you ask her help she will arrange that as she, without any act of her own, was suddenly vindicated by an angel, so will you be. Really it is so, and you will see it.

Put your children and your husband and yourself into God's hand: set them each one in the palm of His hand and bid Him take them and do *His* will. Thus you will have put them into the all-powerful care of illimitable love and wisdom, and all will be well....

I will write again; I will pray for each and all of you, and do write as much as you like and when you like and what you like to me. I will always reply, but perhaps with delay, which I know you will understand....

P.S. The author of enclosed is the most human priest imaginable—you will see that. He is "in process of canonization" (sounds like being made into cheese, somehow!) and working amazing miracles of conversion. Pray to him.

LONDON
17TH MARCH, 1947

Please forgive me for the delay in answering your letter. I was called suddenly away on the day after I got it and when I was just going to answer, to help a person who was flooded in the country, and that has put everything into chaos—you know how it does if an arranged day is suddenly lost when you are busy....

I'm going to leap over to the subject of weariness and fear, because I feel fairly sure that your tiredness, your fear (which I think is not fear, but anxiety) and your feeling of guilt about influencing your children are all from the same root. Clearly there would be, could be, no wrong in influencing your children in the way you know to be for their good; you are made to feel guilty about it by other people. Briefly, I believe the cure for your particular anxiety, and in part the fatigue, will be found in absolutely convincing yourself that what you are doing is good—as it is. Of course you are naturally very tired, working as you must be, and on top of it mental distress—of all things the *most* exhausting. But I've been thinking and thinking about you, and will write tonight to tell you what my thoughts have been—I *really will*: I said last time, I will write again, and did not, I know, but this time I will, but I do not suppose the letter will be posted until tomorrow afternoon. I have to go out now, but this is the first second I have had to write at all since your letter came, and I just feel I must let you know I am thinking of you and praying for you all the time.

I am perfectly certain that it will all come right, but I realize how utterly miserable it is for you now.

Say to the Devil what St. Ignatius did on many occasions: "I did not begin this for you, and I will not end it for you."

By the by, I do know about fear, and the new edition of *This War Is the Passion* (to be called *The Comforting of Christ*) has a section on it. It will be out at the end of April—my other new book, in a few months. But as First Aid for all kinds of fear and anxiety I can recommend ejaculations. Just say again and again, "Sacred Heart of Jesus, I put *all* my trust in you"—and mean it, put Our Lord on His honour. It is quite marvellous how this carries one through. Our Lord likes to be told that you trust Him, and will *not* fail you....

19TH MARCH, 1947

To get into weariness and fear straight away, let me say I am only putting out suggestions, which come as the result of my personal experience and may not apply to you at all. So just take what I say for what it is worth and discard what is worth nothing to you.

I feel that what you call fear is anxiety, an anxious, terrible depression, mixed with a feeling of guilt; and that, however much you reason that you are doing right, this sense of guilt remains and torments; and that you have this kind of anxiety in many, many respects. I do believe that this kind of anxiety, especially when it afflicts a busy person with a clearly sound mind, is the devil's work, and is for one object—namely, to distract your mind from God. Now, in many cases the grossest and most obvious temptations are good enough—a beef-steak on Friday is all the devil requires for his work, or a blatant carnal temptation. But when it comes to someone who has arrived at some measure of strongly conscious spirituality, who has proved a willingness to suffer for God and His truth, the devil must find subtler ways: he must find something which resembles God in this—that it is always present. What could be better than self?—and what more certain to imprison and ultimately obsess a sensitive soul than awareness of something wrong with self? Somehow or other the soul must be made to strive to attain a certain level of holiness, a certain peace or at least untroubledness, *before* abandoning itself to God. It will be held back by this, prevented from seeing more and more the beauty of God. The devil knows that the soul whose heart is fixed on God is lost to Hell, so he must drag the gaze back from God to self. He whispers, through a clergyman or friend, or just your own prompting: "You are doing wrong. Of course you have no peace; you are putting your peace of soul before the happiness of better souls, anyway"—and so on and so on. If you listen, you half agree; you begin again to examine your motives; you let conflict and anxiety rage in you—which is in itself exhausting. A vicious circle begins: you are too tired to pray; you think all consolation has been taken from you, aridity sets in—ultimately you can get a nervous breakdown, if you like!

I feel sure that the treatment is to ignore the suggestions. Even ignore your own soul: keep your mind on God, on His love. For prayer, imagine (only it is not imagining, but true) that at every second of the day about four Masses are being said, and that you, your life, yourself as you are, now in this second, are your offering for the Mass; and offer yourself as you are in union with Our Lord's offering at Mass. Do not wait until you feel not uneasy; do not wait to be doing a more prayerful act; do not wait to feel more unity and completeness: offer yourself, your will to do right, your anxiety about not doing it, your being interrupted just now, the act of taking So-and-so's temperature—all, just as it is, to God. Leave it to God to transform all this into Himself. It's all you've got, and He gave it to you. We are like children whose father has given them a sixpence to buy a birthday present for himself. The father knows the child can't bring him a present costing a pound: he can only give back what he has been given, and whatever scruffy little object he produces, the father loves it, for it is his child's offering of all he *can* offer—and that is only his own gift back again, but back again made more loveable to him by an exchange of their love.

Every time you hesitate, feel anxious, feel guilty, turn to God, say: "*I can't cope with this: I'm doing my best as far as I see it: I put it into your hands to complete.*"

Even the illnesses, the cruel blindness of those you love, the anxiety over the children and the cruelty of this winter, will fall into proportion if you do this—and God, who loves your husband and your children even *more* than you do, knows the moment when it is for their good to flood their minds with light, and *why* it is delayed. He is infinite Wisdom, infinite Power, infinite Love, and if you put them all into His hands, He will make all well, for *them* as much as for you. Drown the devil's voice with the name of Jesus: even when people are talking to you, say it inwardly again and again, until you seem to be breathing it. Don't trust your thoughts of Him: trust Him....

23RD MARCH, 1947

Thank you more than I can say for those miraculously lovely snowdrops. When I opened that box the wonder of them just took my breath away.

It was really most sweet of you to have sent them, and it must have taken you hours and hours to pick and pack them so beautifully. They arrived perfectly fresh and smelling exquisitely and now, in water here, seem to get fresher and more alive every hour. I divided them with friends, and yet we all (three of us) have our rooms just filled with them, and I have a great bowl of them under my crucifix which it is a delight to look at.

I did so want you to have this letter thanking you first thing on Monday morning, but you will not. I had planned to write early this afternoon, but had arranged a tea-party of converted Jews at 4 o'clock. The first of them, however, arrived at 2 o'clock, and the last to go left only 8.15, after the last post out.

So I was thwarted. But how those Jews do have to suffer for their Christianity—they are persecuted by their own people and get very little welcome from Christians: neither, oddly enough, do they usually want to know each other! ...

4TH APRIL, 1947

Your wonderful parcel arrived yesterday, absolutely intact and absolutely wonderful. How astonishingly good of you, and I have never seen anything so Easterish, so completely new life and loveliness risen out of darkness.

I was amazed at seeing eggs, and I have hidden them and am going to put them on the table on Easter morning (I always cook the breakfast), and they will be such a surprise and delight to my friend, and consequently a double delight to me. I have potted the primroses: what an inspiration to send roots!—you must have a great understanding of flowers and earth. Those pussy willows are too lovely for words—what a tender blue sheen is on them, as if still, in London, they are reflecting the blue skies they grew under.

Thank you again and again and again.

Now about the problem of the children.... I am certain that you are mistaken in thinking that you have a "double duty." You have not got a duty to your soul and another separate duty to your children; your duty to your children *is* your duty to your soul.

I know what agony it is to have to cause any suffering to your children, and there is another aspect of it—namely, that it is very likely indeed that you would in fact cause them far *more* suffering ultimately, by failing God. They are old enough to know, and to remember very bitterly later on, that if you don't go on now, it will be failing to do what you know to be the right and true thing for them (and for a *mistaken* idea of their good)....

But the fact is, every mother is first and foremost a mother of Christ. Your children are Christ-children, mystical Christs. Every baptized child is first of all God's child, and every Christian who comes into the world comes into it to be "another Christ." Every mother, therefore, can look to Our Lady, as mother of Christ, for light and for what to do. Now the fact is, because her only child was Christ and had come to do His Father's will, she was able to face the Passion, and never tried to hold Him back or spare Him. That she loved Him is proved by the fact that she followed Him to the cross, and could even stand and watch His crucifixion; but her love was able to bear it because she realized that He was, first of all, God's Christ.

Your children are here to be Christs. Each has her part in the redemption of the world, and what she has to suffer because you are doing God's will is part of her Christhood (or Christ-life, I should say).

Actually, if you drew back it would not make the situation better now. Your nerves would break and, guessing rather freely, I think your husband's would get much worse. He, without recognizing it, would feel guilty, and nothing makes a man, especially a possessive man, more inclined to hurt someone than the fact that he has wronged them—that their very meekness is a reproach to him. It is better that, since rage he will, he rages because you have done right than because you have done wrong!—better for you all.

I have the fixed idea that if you can get down to your own guilt feeling, and convince yourself that you are doing right, not to your own soul only, but to everyone, you will find that as the sense of guilt falls from you, your husband's nerves will improve too. It is very likely indeed that a far deeper buried guilt feeling is what is wrong with him.

I have suffered all my life from neurotic guilt myself, and I know the havoc it plays. For your children's sake too, you should think about it. I will so gladly help you to get over it—and you can, you know. One thing essential, though, is the real sacraments. I was first told this is a *medical* fact by a Jewish-born, atheist doctor, and oddly enough was told it again last week by a doctor who is a converted Jew, John Friedman (he has written a magnificent book, *The Conversion of Israel*).

I am quite sure you must go straight on, and remember this: It's not you putting your soul before your children, but you saving your soul *for* your children.

You know they are first of all God's children: each of them is to Him as Christ, as His only child. It is not a matter of His *allowing* them to suffer for your soul, or for their own good: He only allows them to suffer what He knows to be essential for *them* and for their own greatest good. Each of them is in His hand; He knows and loves them even more than you do, knows what to do for them. Your love *is* but His love for them; you must comfort yourself by knowing this.

… Now I wish you a happy Easter. Even knowing its shadows for you, I shall pray that Our Lord in His own way will give you the joy of Easter in your heart.

You know, you should not let being a Catholic make a *separation*. You speak as if you think you are abandoning your children—but no: you are still all loving Our Lord. You can still be, *should* still be, united in His love.

7TH APRIL, 1947

First of all I want to tell you how we enjoyed our Easter breakfast and blessed you for it. I hid the eggs from my friend and made a nest with some of the moss in your box and put them in it, and also put the primroses growing in a big bowl, and now they are flowering wonderfully and look as if they are made of light: the pussy willow palms are coming out and hanging tiny green chains and causing me to say I know not how many prayers a day for you.

Now I want to get down to the guilt feeling with all its fears and difficulties.

My belief is that you suffer from nervous anxiety—that you have this tendency to *feel* guilty, when your reason assures you that you are not, and that you very readily allow other people to make you feel guilty. Thousands of people suffer from this, and it expresses itself in countless different ways, sometimes in scrupulosity, sometimes in obsessional neurosis, continual handwashing, sometimes waking in the night in the grip of nameless, shapeless fear—the most awful form of fear that there is. There are also many, many secondary causes: unhappy childhoods in disunited families, all sorts of early experiences, and, besides that, possibly inherited race consciousness—I mean inherited anxieties of a whole race. But though these secondary causes are as far back as the average psychiatrist will take a patient—at least, they are as a rule—they are not really the cause. The primary, real cause of them all, and of the neurosis of our generation generally, and the reason why secondary causes, in early childhood, in adolescence and during any crisis in life, are so powerful to afflict us, is our dislocation from God. A thing which is in the last resort spiritual in its origin can and does express itself in other ways. It appears as a nervous, even a physical disorder, but these disorders, these psychological troubles and nervous troubles are really symptoms of a spiritual state: they are symptoms just as, for example, faintness is a symptom of heart trouble: but the trouble itself can be caused by a great many different things—by, for example, congenital muscular weakness or vitamin deficiency. The physical organ will act in the same way for many different causes.

Now, owing to original sin, we are all a bit dislocated from God, and in so far as we lose sight of, or fall short of, His will for us, for each one of us individually, we develop neurosis, anxiety, etc. Added to that, in England at all events, most are starved of sacramental life, which…is essential to balance and to psychological health.…

Now, don't think I'm trying to tell you you are a neurasthenic or psychopath. No, but many—in fact, most—normal people have some measure of neurosis in this way—a sense of guilt and anxiety which, if they will face it, is founded, not in real wrong they have done or are doing, but in themselves. In fact, they are looking round for *something* to attach their guilt to, in order to seek relief.

It is like someone who has a continual pain, who seeks for diagnosis, and may be relieved to discover some actual disorder because so it can be cured. The confessional is haunted by poor people suffering from this neurosis; they go to confession thinking to get a *feeling* of relief. They don't get it, and start wondering if they have confessed everything, search their souls, torment themselves, want to make endless, less and less real confessions. They are seeking relief—just that. Now, the interesting thing is that anxiety of this kind hardly ever attaches to real guilt. It is frequently found in murderers: a man in America who murdered a child and felt very little sorrow for it, wept over his untidiness! Now of course it is a grand thing for the devil to fasten on and use; a great sinner can be kept from suffering for his *real* guilt by it.

To come back to you. If you have this anxiety complex (I have it myself, by the by), obviously with all the opposition, plus physical tiredness, etc., everything you are going through is going to fasten it on to all of your acts and decisions, making you feel that whatever you do is guilty and wrong, and so leading you to a never-ending, dangerous state of indecision and hesitation which would spell ruin for you.

What is the cure?

Well, absolute abandonment to God's will. In point of fact, there can be no doubt that it *is* His will for you to accept the truth as He has revealed it and as you in His grace have seen it to be. There can be no doubt at all that it is His will for you to receive Him in the sacraments, and all your scruples about your children are answered in Our Lord's own words, in His own voice, in the Gospel. The answer frankly is a hard one, but its hardness fades when you realize the certainty of *His own love* making all well for those dear to you—so much dearer to Him.

What you have to do is to say: "I am a sinner; I do deserve to feel anxious and guilty, but I am *not* guilty in becoming a Catholic. I am doing it because I sincerely believe it is the right thing, even if I *feel* again and again that it is wrong. I accept the discomfort of feeling uneasy and I am going straight on ignoring my feeling."

Put your faith in God all the time, and you will find that as soon as you cease to have any inward hesitation, your husband, without knowing why himself, will be much less antagonistic. I can't explain why in this letter, or I'll miss the post.

But what I want to say is: attack your guilt feeling as a guilt feeling; do not let the devil trick you into looking for relief by any side-tracking. You can't get rid of an anxiety feeling in a day, but I really believe that even within an hour, if you will face it and see what it is, you can so immobilize it that you can make it ineffective in hindering your logical actions or in upsetting your personal relationships. Naturally, perfect peace in the family won't come at once, but it will *begin* to come at once....

Westminster Hospital
22nd April, 1947
(*Written in pencil.*)

I can't thank you enough for all your trouble and kindness in sending me the *most beautiful brown eggs*, which my friend has brought here; they are marked with my name and will be given to me for most delicious meals.

You ought not to have troubled, and *please* do not send any more: these are lovely and I appreciate your kindness deeply, but I shall not be able to eat more than these while I am here, and no nurse or friend will accept one, much as I would like to share them. They insist on keeping them for me, and even "Sister" says I am spoilt and have enough. I do thank you so very much.

I came in more suddenly than I expected...and had the operation on Friday. It was more extensive than was expected, but perfectly successful, and I am recovering with wonderful rapidity....

I am so delighted to think that you are either received already or about to be—have been praying for you, and will.

You are not without human help, but without visible (to you) human help! You must take great comfort in knowing that you are now in the fullest communion not only with all living Catholics, but with the saints in heaven and the Holy Souls, in a great unity of deep and tender and detailed love—no soul that in the heart of God is *not* now helping you and belonging to you, and no soul in purgatory or in heaven lacks the power of a nearly or quite perfected love.

I cannot yet write much; I haven't got to the sitting-up stage, so it is awkward; but I will write again when I can. Meantime, thank you very much, and I send you my most joyful and loving wishes for your reception into the Church....

WESTMINSTER HOSPITAL
27TH APRIL, 1947
(*In pencil.*)

This will very likely be my last chance to write to you before you are received, so I will say how very much I will be thinking of you and praying for you; and, besides the comfort of knowing that despite anything you do or do not *feel*, Our Lord will be for evermore abiding in you and your constant strength, you will also have the constant friendship of St. Catherine of Siena, who was at one time my *only* Catholic friend!

Oh, don't worry about your not feeling any consolation. You know that when Our Lord gives consolation we should be glad and grateful, but equally when He does not. Offer yourself to Him as if you were the unfeeling humble substance of bread, as near to nothing as a substance can be, and *He* will say the words of consecration and transform your life to His. Even then the transformation may not be evident to your senses or feelings, but it will happen, just as mysteriously and invisibly to sense or feeling, perhaps, as the change from common bread to Christ's body in the Host; but also, *really*, and to *God's* eyes, clearly visible.

Naturally you are tired. You are emotionally tired, and tired-out emotions can no more feel sweetness than tired eyes can see clearly—unless, indeed, it is a special grace of feeling. But the great and wonderful grace isn't feeling, but surrendering your will and all you are, nervous exhaustion included, to God. Have no fear at all; He will do everything else necessary for you and those you love.

As to "missing Mass"—there is *no* obligation to attend Sunday Mass when you are so far from a church. It would be a joy to you if you could, but it may be God's way of getting *you* hard on to the basic, elemental essentials of His love, and of showing your family that Catholicism is first of all between God and the soul. I've no doubt that if you try to be spiritually present at all the Masses going on all over the world on Sundays, very soon Our Lord will solve the problem for you.

"Mortal sins in your own mind" just don't matter, because they aren't real. Surrender to the Church's motherly wisdom, which is Christ's voice on earth, and which is always lenient, and first of all for the weakest: then you will find loving obedience a healing balm for scruples like that.

I am getting on well, and want to get home. I am very, very tired, and trying to do things is not so easy now, but really all that can be done for me here is done, and wonderfully done.…

Anyhow, I shall be with you in prayer on Wednesday, and I know that all is well with you, in spite of your not feeling it to be so. Go on telling yourself "Under me are the everlasting arms," for that is and always will be true.

Westminster Hospital
1st May, 1947

The primroses and really celestial violets and ferns like naughty boys arrived on St. Catherine's feast (I think the day before), and in so fresh a condition that the delighted nurses who saw them opened regarded it as a miracle! To add to the miracle, they are *still* as fresh and radiant and lovely, and are a most wonderful joy, both to me and everyone else here. Thank you very, very much.

I was indeed sorry about the postponement of your reception. I am sure, however, that St. Catherine will take you under her special care and give you her wonderful friendship all the same.…

You are probably going through all sorts of changing reactions about this delay, but next Wednesday will soon be here, and I feel sure you will know far deeper peace after it—not unbroken, but of a quality to build up your strength against the difficult times, whether they come from inside or out. Do remember when you go to confession that in this case, almost more than any other, feeling isn't the main thing. Do *not* worry if you feel that you made a bad confession, forgot something, were not, or did not feel, sorry, and so on—none of it matters; the main thing about confession is that it is, as Holy Communion is, a receiving of Our Lord, another infusion of His life, a communion with Him: that is the great point, *not* your accuracy of memory and exactitude in listing sins! If you intended to do your best when confessing, nothing else matters to God. What's forgotten is forgiven with the rest, and if you feel good or not after it, you've come closer to Our Lord and He to you, and, *knowing* this, *accepting* it, and ignoring your worries, will bring you to the real lasting peace. I may be being impertinent and giving you unnecessary and unwanted advice. I am risking it because I have seen so many sensitive people, especially those with your temperament, suffer intensely and unnecessarily over this, and Anglican converts quite often have a wrong idea of confession. They have usually, perhaps without realizing it, used it more from the point of view of personal relief and spiritual direction than from the point of view which is the really sacramental one—direct contact with Christ. I shall be thinking of you and praying for you very much, especially on Wednesday, and eager to know that you have been received....

By this morning's post I heard of a Jewish family being suddenly converted, just at the height of their persecution of the (until now) solitary convert in the family, one son: they are all being instructed! You see miracles do happen; this must have been simply an answer to prayer. The same thing may happen to your husband: never give up asking God for it, and Our Lady. God can do it so easily!

Please forgive my delay in thanking you for the lovely flowers. I have been wanting to write ever since I got them, but had some rather hard days, and also have run out of envelopes, so can't post this until my friend brings some, which I hope she will today.

Now I must say goodbye for today. If the waiting seems hard, think of the two thousand years that Our Lord has been waiting in the Blessed Sacrament, longing for His Communion with you. The glorious thing is that your First Communion will be a first Communion for Him too!

819 Nell Gwynn House
19th May, 1947

Thank you so very, very much for your letter on the day of your reception and for the simply lovely cowslips, which arrived in such a glorious condition of living yellow light. I also noticed for the first time what a peculiarly lovely delicate green their stems are—what an astonishing *variety* of greens God does use. I am always dismayed at the thought of the hours you must have spent gathering flowers for me, and afraid it may have kept you up late into the night at the family mending or washing-up. The cowslips are so lovely, though, that selfishly I rejoice in having them. I was simply overjoyed by your description of your reception—so glad that after all the painful delays, which you bore so heroically and beautifully, you were given a little visible heaven, and a memory that will be strength to you whenever you draw on it, all through your life....

6th June, 1947

... I must tell you first that the bluebells were untold joy, and I noticed that everyone who came leaned down and buried their faces in them, in a gesture that was eloquent with unconscious humility. I always put flowers that grow low on the ground, low in my room, so that one looks down on them as one would were they growing, and seeing the instinct in everyone to bow down to them, I wondered whether country people have more humility than townspeople. The people in towns probably have forgotten or never seen most of the manifestations of the splendour and mystery and the loveliness of God. They have built up things that hide the reflection of His face from them—though when I am here[†] (note how contra-suggestive I am) I feel that the incessant efforts of the people here to draw one's attention to this or that detail of nature is a

---

[†] Written from the country.

positive distraction: one has so intensely the sense of all nature, taken as a whole—sky, earth, blossom, stars and sun and moon and rain and dew, all together—being a thin veil on the eternal light, or a faint pulse of everlasting light. In London, one flower brings the whole wonder and mystery of this shining veil into one's room, but in the country it seems to me one wants to receive it whole, as one receives Communion, and it is difficult not to become irritated by being asked to see it in terms of gardening or the interesting habits of ants—however, from the point of view of gardeners and Fabre fans, it is otherwise!

... I must try to answer your request of knowing what to do.... Actually it is difficult to say: I think you want to "do something," just as one wants to hold a rosary or crucifix in one's hand, to try to concentrate the illimitable love and gratitude to a point. Some people are in danger when they start to "do," and forget how infinitely more important it is to *be*. But I am sure this danger does not exist for you....

But it seems to me...the really essential thing is to practice, as a *positive art*, to see and serve Christ in *everyone* in the house—your own family: almost, though I know how queer this sounds, to say your prayers (inwardly) to them! Or—and this may be an easier way to start—concentrate on the fact that Christ is *in* you, and that you have to give Him to them: that you, through your own presence and relationship to them, have to give them their Communion with Him, although they do not know this, saying "May the Body and Blood of Our Lord Jesus Christ bring you to life everlasting," or "Receive Jesus Christ" every time you do anything for them, or restrain a word or sigh of impatience, or say anything to them. This is a practice which, though it is not sensational and takes (often) years before you see any results, is very apostolic, and, besides that, brings you tremendous peace. If, apart from this work of *being Christ* in your own world, you have in fact some specific vocation to do some particular thing for Him, this will, in His own time, be made known to you, either by an irresistible inner compulsion or else by so obvious a chain of circumstances that they *can* only be regarded as a finger pointing clearly in one direction. Even one's own psychological difficulties and deficiencies of personality are, as soon as one's will is wholly abandoned to God (and He has always known if at a certain point it *will* be), means of almost compelling one to walk in one's true vocation. Most so-called nervous breakdowns are only the collapse of a personality trying to be other than that which they must be to fulfil God's plan for them. A real contemplative breaks down if he tries to excel in action, and one intended for an active vocation breaks down if he attempts to be a pure contemplative; and, in both cases, the certain cure is to see God's guiding finger and walk wholeheartedly in the way it points.

For the moment, the precious and only *now*, you alone are the bearer of the Blessed Sacrament into your own little world. You are the monstrance, the priest giving Communion, the Real Presence, to your husband, your children and your friends; and the reason why, or one reason why, Christ has given Himself to you, is because He wishes to be with them, and can be with them, as things are, only through you. This is an astonishing thought, as every thought about the Blessed Sacrament is, if you bring an ounce of courage and realism to it.

Do you know the life of Charles de Foucauld?—a great symbol of many souls today. He was murdered by an Arab in the desert; there he had set up a hermit's life, a little solitary kind of monastery. He had never, in spite of the strongest possible urge to go into the desert and found a mission there, made any converts there (or anywhere, I think!), but he knew and said that his life, which was apparently fruitless, was wholly worth while, for one thing alone—namely, to take the Blessed Sacrament into the desert. He knew that if Our Lord was there in the Blessed Sacrament, He (Our Lord) would do there whatever He had come to do; that *He* is irresistible; and Charles de Foucauld did not think the sacrifice of everything, including his own life, too much to give for this end. It is precisely the same with us. There is nothing too much to do, in order to bring Christ in the Blessed Sacrament, as the sacramental life of our souls, into our own world, or home.

It is an interesting fact that the Order Charles de Foucauld founded never came to anything in his lifetime. If it ever had any membership at all, it soon died out; and yet now it has suddenly started to flourish.

Many people are joining, and it is obviously going to flower, at this moment of intense need, into a living apostolate to the Arabs—a matter surely closely connected in the divine plan with the imminent (I think) conversion of the Jews....

LONDON
27TH JULY, 1947

Thank you very much for your letter. It is obvious I am thinking of you this afternoon, and at 3–3.30 I shall be praying for you to the Holy Spirit. It is enough to say the names of the Holy Spirit to receive grace; Spirit of Light, Spirit of Truth, Spirit of Love, Spirit of Life!

The living stream of grace, that will pour into your soul and fill it with undying life, so passes anything one can say about joy or blessedness or courage that it is better on such a day to say nothing, but instead to praise and thank God for you....

23RD SEPTEMBER, 1947

Regarding pain and death and the fear of it for those dear to us and ourselves.

The fear does not show any want of faith; faith does not ask of us to be inhuman. Our Lord experienced all the fears you are experiencing, in the Agony in the Garden; moreover, He showed, by weeping in public, extreme grief over death, even in the case of Lazarus, whom He was about to raise from the dead. He never rebuked anyone for mourning over the dead; on the contrary, He was so moved by their grief that He several times restored the dead to life—the daughter of Jairus, the widow's son, etc.—from sheer compassion.

From this fact one may learn that first of all there is not the least imperfection or want of faith in the feeling of fear in this way, or in shrinking from these things. Actually, since pain and death are both primarily results of sin, there is something essentially right in hating and fearing them in themselves. But a second deduction from what I have said above about Our Lord is that His compassion is such that if He can spare us these sufferings, even by a miracle, He will; and from this, yet another, and the most important conclusion of all: namely, God (for Christ is God)—God will never allow any pain or illness or death for anyone, *unless* it is essential and necessary for our ultimate joy: unless, because of the multitudinous circumstances of our life, known only to God (not known to anyone else, even ourselves), this particular suffering has become the *only* way through which we can arrive at ultimate lasting happiness.

So we can pray with great confidence because we *know* that God Himself *wants* to spare us; and if He can, without taking away from our final happiness, He will.

I think it is very helpful to reflect that God loves those whom we love, far *more* than we do—infinitely more. We love at all only because our hearts dimly reflect His. We know and realize a fragment of what goes on in the hearts of our nearest and dearest: God knows every nerve and fibre.

I have personally found it helpful to accept fear, to say, "Yes, I am afraid: for as long as this suspense (or whatever it is) lasts, I *shall* be afraid. I accept it as perfectly just and right." Some people might not be helped by this thought, but I have been, profoundly and often, myself.…

30TH APRIL, 1948

… Your own troubles are really very sad indeed; I do feel very deeply for you. It certainly seems that prayer is the only help—that and taking each trial separately, trying not to look miles ahead with the overwhelming picture of years of succeeding crises to weigh you down. Prayer does bring such amazing answers that it is reasonable to hope that every separate crisis may be the last and happiness may come very suddenly, when you least expect it.

… Do you find help from the rosary? I find just holding on to it, even, helps. Of course, some would say that is mere superstition, but it isn't if it symbolizes holding on to God, as it does for me. I have been visiting a girl once a week for a doctor; the girl was a baffling nerve case. She used to have about three attacks a day resembling acute attacks of St. Vitus's dance, and followed by palpitations of so violent a nature that the doctors marvelled that her heart could stand up to it.… She had been previously two years in hospital and had seen every specialist, but no one could diagnose her case and she just went on getting worse. She had no religion, and her only reaction to God—a very vague idea to her—was fear and aversion.

I gave her a rosary and told her to try to say *something* with it in her hand—her own prayer—or say nothing, but *mean* to hold on to God. From the hour she took the rosary into her hand she has been better, and is now almost cured.… I do not attribute this cure wholly to the rosary—at least, not directly, as the doctor tried a new cure, based on a guess of her own and as a desperate chance, and I think she had found the right clue; but I think her finding it is all part of the answer to the girl's first prayer with the rosary.… Her mind has flowered too, literally changed from a narrow self-obsessed mind to a big, objective, clever and loving one.

Shortly, everyone (Catholics, I mean) will be starting to make novenas to the Holy Spirit in preparation for Pentecost; it is an old custom called the Novena for Light: groups of friends adopt one another's intentions and pray for them in their own novenas. These novenas to the Holy Spirit bring streams of light and grace. Let us adopt one another's intentions and make the novena.…

It is very natural that you feel indispensable; you *are*, in the natural order; but you must comfort yourself by continually reminding yourself that your children are first of all God's children. He loves them more than you do, and He will never for a split second remove His tender care from them. You can be certain that He will always look after them, and although you can't *see* His wisdom, you can be certain that what He allows to happen *is* part of His infinite wisdom for them. But how well

I know how hard it is to believe that, and how utterly baffling things seem....

My book is a spiritual book. It is on the subject of the "redemptive childhood," which I believe to be the special kind of holiness of our century. It was inspired by Clare—at least, in a way it was, but on the first night of the war, and my first night in a First Aid Post, an unnecessarily macabre one in a rat-infested basement, this book, or some strange presentiment of it, came into my mind. It was as if the Holy Innocents of Bethlehem whom Herod murdered were flocking around our heads, singing shrilly with joy, and the phrase "Passio Infantis Christi" kept echoing in my mind....

London
3rd January, 1949

... Your letter telling me you had offered your Mass for darling little Clare moved me as nothing else could have done; and the curious thing is that I was—yes—*compelled*, as if by my angel, to pray for you and your family almost all the time. I kept trying to speak of others too, including Clare of course, but I had a sudden feeling that I was bidden to pray for you—so your name was woven all through the Midnight Mass like a litany.

You speak of losing the closeness (physical) of those who have been a help to you. This is so often the experience of people who are being united to God. I think that it is only when everyone who helps us to know God has gone that we do at last realize the reality of just ourselves, alone with God. This is a reality, although the Communion of Saints—and sinners—in Him is one too. When I say "has gone," I don't mean that everyone who helps will be taken away, though usually *some* are, when they have done what God meant them to; but I mean that for a long time, without realizing it and probably as part of God's plan for us, we are basing our knowledge of God, even our approach to Him, on other people's conception of Him. In the presence of a very holy priest, for example, we can sometimes literally *feel his* love of God like the warmth of a fire, and the reflection of that glowing fire radiates from our own soul, as if it were our own love, which it is not entirely, though it is a beautiful lesson in love. Again, sometimes someone speaks of God in words which so truly express what we had felt vaguely, or *wanted* to think or feel about God, that we really think that person's idea of God is our own. Then there are books which support us like swimming wings do in the sea, and we are carried along on the love of the writers of the books. All these things are part of our communion with one another, and friendships, affections and books, that flow with God's love and cause us to flow back, are real graces. But sooner or later, if we are to be united to Him in this life, they will cease, at all events for a time, to help. This person will go away, that one will seem to fail us, the spirituality of so-and-so, which once stimulated us, will, we know not why, do so no longer. We will outgrow such-and-such a book, another will lose its magic. Now for the first time we shall not only have to discover God for ourselves, metaphorically, see Him with our own eyes, but we shall have to be there in His presence as ourselves, stripped of everyone else, without any reflected light or feeling from anyone else. This is the moment when our experience of God becomes the very core and truth of our being. It is, of course, a painful experience too; all real self-knowing is that—it *must* be; but knowing ourselves, not only as we really are, but as we really are in *God's presence*—well, it sometimes seems to me that in this experience, more than in any other suffering life can give to us, we begin our purgatory on earth....

    I am glad you liked the tiny Our Lady I sent. I wanted to make you a larger one, but two considerations stopped me. One was that it might aggravate your difficulties if I put you into the position of putting up statues, "graven images," etc., in your home, so that one small enough to keep on you might prove more tactful; secondly, as I had hardly ever an hour in twenty-four to carve in my room, for *months* before Christmas, I had to make something which I could carry in my pocket and do at odd moments and in odd places, with a small knife and a tiny engraving tool. The result is, I know, very crude, but you are so charitable, and overlook the faults.…

London
23rd January, 1949

It appalls me to realize that so long has passed since you wrote to me, and a letter that does need an answer. But now I must hope that your guardian angel has helped instead of me; he (your angel) is far better able to. I always ask my angel to speak to the guardian angels of the people I want to reach quickly.…

I do feel very deeply for you in all the terrible troubles you have to face, and with so little help or sympathy. I did not mean by my last letter that we ought not to look to others to help and comfort us, for, as I said before, and you remember, Our Lord did so in Gethsemane, and on the way to Calvary He let Simon even be *compelled* to help Him to carry the Cross. But what I was trying to say is, that if someone (like a priest one is getting dependent on) is becoming, perhaps without our realizing it, a sort of middle-man between us and God, so that we are never, as it were, alone with—and wholly *ourselves*—alone with God, and know Him directly as He wishes *us* to know Him, not through the medium of someone else's thoughts or experiences of Him—*then, that* "help" is likely to be removed, at least for a time.

Of course you are right to want the help of others in general, and in the carrying of your cross; and in admitting your need you are more, not less, "a Christ." It is really impossible for *anyone*, priest or other, to tell you what to do about the impasse at home, but I wish you had a kind, holy old priest who could strengthen you by his understanding and comfort. Such a person in your life might do so much to make it easier for you to cope with things.

Very often it seems that the more we pray for something we want which seems good and happy to us, the more hopeless the thing seems to become! But I heard a sermon by an old priest in our local church the other day which seemed to help, so I will relay it to you. He spoke about the Wedding Feast at Cana—the miracle of the changing of the water into wine. He made three points, all amazingly real and simple; only the third and last is the one I want to stress for you, but I will tell you the others, as they are also interesting and very consoling. (1) People say that the miracle was done for a trivial cause and are therefore scandalized, but the fact is that the host was embarrassed, and that, on a unique occasion—his child's marriage—and to God, the feelings, embarrassment, etc., of any of His children is *not* trivial; it counts enormously to Him and is worth a miracle! (2) Our Lord usually turned up with some of His friends; He probably brought a number to the wedding, which was *why* the wine ran out so early. Our Lord is the sort of person who is too courteous and considerate and too good-mannered to allow His coming to be a disaster to anyone! The third point (the one for you and me particularly), namely, the good wine, the "best wine," was saved (so the steward said in astonishment) to the last—not given first, as was expected and usual. This, the priest said, is God's way; He hears our prayer, above all if we get Our Lady (as in this case) to say it for us; He answers it; but we often don't know this, until, when it seems that everything is finished, and no hope left—right at the last, we suddenly get the answer, which is unimaginably better than anything we could expect! ...

2ND MARCH, 1949
ASH WEDNESDAY

... As to your Lent, of course I am in no way entitled to give you advice; I can only tell you my own experience. A mass of good resolutions, I think, are apt to end up in disappointment and to make one depressed. Also direct fault-uprooting: it makes one concentrate too much on self, and that can be so depressing. The only resolution I have ever found works is: "Whenever I want to think of myself, I will think of God." Now, this does not mean, "I will make a long meditation on God," but just some short sharp answer, so to speak, to my thought of self, in God. For example:

"I am lonely, misunderstood, etc."

"The loneliness of Christ at His trial; the misunderstanding even of His closest friends."

Or:

"I have made a fool of myself."

"Christ mocked—He felt it; He put the mocking *first* in foretelling His Passion—'The Son of Man shall be mocked, etc.'—made a fool of, before all whom He loved."

Or:

"I can't go on, unhelped."

"Christ couldn't. He couldn't carry the cross without help; He was grateful for human sympathy—Mary Magdalene—His words on that occasion—other examples as they suggest themselves—just pictures that flash through the mind." This practice becomes a habit, and it is the habit which has saved me from despair!

You need not fear loving Our Lady more than God; nothing pleases Our Lord more than that you love His mother. Did He not actually give her to John to take His place, and John to her? She is the best way to Him, and it is only *because* of Him that we do love her. What else you say, about Our Lord as a baby and child is, curiously enough, answered fully, in so far as I can answer it, in my new book…so I will leave it at that. But it's all all right. Different people have different approaches to Christ. He has become all things—infant, child, man—so that we all can approach Him in the way easiest for us. The best is to use *that* way to our heart's content, and not to trouble about any other.

28TH JUNE, 1949

… About mortal sin. I am sure you could not commit one if you tried! It requires *grave matter*—and that does really mean grave matter; *deliberate intention*—i.e. you know it is mortal sin and fully intend to do it, and to commit mortal sin, in defiance of God. *Full consent*—you must be perfectly free to give full consent—not under strong compulsion through influence or fear, or not sober, or in abnormal condition of any sort; and then, fully, deliberately, consent to do it. *Full knowledge*—that is, full knowledge of the enormity of the evil, what it really means, and so on.

You see, it isn't easy for anyone; for someone who has the *least* love of God, it is nearly impossible.

But the devil loves to distract one from God's love and mercy by worry about sin. The only cure for this worry is to concentrate, not on self-perfection, but on the love and tenderness of God. The best prayer, this—*Veni [Sancte Spiritus]*—in the Missal, on Whitsunday.

7TH AUGUST, 1949

… I do know all about the terrible depression you speak of, as I suffer from it too, and have done so ever since I was nine years old or so, on and off; and I realize that while the attack lasts, *nothing* can either stop it or relieve it.

But one is not helpless, all the same. First of all, there are natural causes which aggravate it terribly, and one has a duty to try to use what natural means one can to lessen the attacks. The greatest *natural* cause of them is, quite simply, fatigue.

You must start by re-ordering your life, in order to use your vitality and your psychological energy more economically. I am certain that you are living above your psychological income, and have done so for years.

You can't, at the moment, alter your circumstances, but you can alter something in yourself. You live every moment of the day at top speed, too fast, crowding too much emotion, anxiety, even good will, into every moment. You ought to slow down. God has given you a pretty good hint with your foot. But it is not enough to work at half-speed; you must deliberately practice thinking at half-speed, praying at half-speed, talking at halfspeed. I should suggest resolving to say not more than one Our Father and one Hail Mary a day, and go on saying it all day, dwelling slowly, deliberately, first on every phrase, later over every word. Do not be put off or perturbed by distractions. Just go on where you left off when you think of it. On days when even a kind of "free association" of thoughts about these two prayers fails you, slow up by taking deep breaths between each word, and just repeat the prayers, word by word, breathing deeply between each word as often as you like.

Now—and this will seem harsh advice—when some joy comes your way, and you feel really happy or fervent, slow that down too; don't let it rip, put the brake on and take it very quietly. The reason for this is that people of your temperament often exhaust themselves as much in letting out all their sail in happy things as they do through unhappy ones; and because they have tired themselves out in, say, a day of fervour, the fatigue which follows is increased in proportion, and the fatigue sets the measure of the intensity of the depression.

Next, bring all the rest you can into enduring the very real and great sufferings of your family life. Stop trying to think out a solution for the moment: there isn't one. One day there may be; God will then show it to you. In the meantime, accept it all as *being* the big thing for God and His Church that He asks of you—that, and the depression too. You will find the relief of merely accepting, instead of struggling, wonderful; and I include in this, accepting anything in yourself, during the crisis, which seems to you a failure or fault. Don't *exonerate* yourself, but just say you are sorry, briefly, to God, and add that your name is dirt—that's what is to be expected from you—but you're sorry, you are forgiven, and it is over.

During the war I was simply terrified by air raids, and it was my lot to be in every one that happened in London—sometimes on the roofs of these flats, sometimes in the hospital.... I tried to build up my courage by reason and prayer, etc. Then one day I realized quite suddenly: As long as I try not to be afraid I shall be worse, and I shall show it one day and break; what God is asking of me, to do for suffering humanity, is to *be* afraid, to accept it and put up with it, as one has to put up with pain (if it's not druggable) or anything else. I am not going to get out of *any* of the suffering. From the time the siren goes until the All Clear, I am going to be simply frightened stiff, and that's what I've got to do for the world—offer *that* to God, because it is *that* and nothing else which He asks of me.

From that hour it became easy. I *was* terrified, but I was also perfectly conscious of being held in God's hands; before, I was too tensed to feel them. From the moment I just let go, I *knew* I was held up, and there was nothing more to worry about.

I am sure that what God is asking of you *is* your suffering; this brings you into immediate communion with all the martyrs, known and unknown, suffering today for the Faith. It is, if offered in reparation, the deepest possible form of contemplation and the most powerful apostolate. It is the very power of Christ, standing as Priest and Redeemer before God.

All that you speak of—fear of death, anxiety about sin, etc.—can be included in this suffering. Don't try to mitigate it; accept it, offer it for the world to God. He will take it away when He wants to.

There is no want of faith in fear of death—in fact, it is right to fear it and shrink from it, since death has come into the world through sin. It is against nature and against God's will; the instinctive shrinking from it which all healthy-minded people feel, is right and goes to prove how we all are really made in the image of God. It is also part of our redemption to fear it. It *is* a punishment. But the fear can gradually be tempered by hope, and reduced as we grow in Christhood and in love for God, because Christ, by surrendering Himself in His human nature to death, has made it not only a punishment but a doorway to life. Also, *He* has already died *your* death and overcome it!

On the purely natural plane, fear of death usually shows natural vitality and health. As we get weaker and iller, we fear it less and less, and hundreds of doctors, priests and nurses testify the fact that death, when it comes, is nearly *always* merciful and easy. For a Catholic, the Holy Viaticum brings Our Lord Himself to help and makes it easier still, and sheer physical weakness helps!

But no reasoning helps about this fear, I know. Like all the rest, the best is to accept it.

God is showing you a very great favour in giving you such big suffering for His children. I am sure you are among those chosen few who are being asked to reach out invisibly to all those who are in such bitter need of spiritual help today—and this is so *much* more than any specific little good work or "Catholic Action" you could do.

Accept it all as Our Lord did His own Passion in Gethsemane. He experienced all this fear, asked to be let off, and when He wasn't He surrendered every fibre of His being to God's will. Repeat *His* prayer, in His power, in the power of His *risen* love, which is yours if you choose to use it: "Not my will—but thine."

Of course I realize how heroic all this sounds and what a *lot* it asks of your poor human nature, but in it is the seed of peace: and do not forget that, in our Christ-life as in His historical life, the Resurrection *must* follow swiftly on the crucifixion.

London
19th September, 1949

About your other difficulty, about Communion: of course I don't think it is trivial, it is very real indeed.

Accept the nerves as a trial from God, but do what you can to deal with them quietly so that they will *not* prevent your Communion. If, however, they sometimes do, accept that humbly too, make a spiritual Communion, and when you get a chance, go to Communion on an extra day (weekday).

I should try to take a cup of a sedative called Sedebrol before bed, go to bed rather earlier if you can, have your Sedebrol and then lie in bed reading—not spiritual books, but detective fiction, until you fall asleep. If this fails, ask your doctor's advice. Clearly, and not surprisingly, your nerves are suffering from the strain of it all, and you need general treatment, to get anywhere near the root of the trouble. But above *all* you need to get away, for at least a month, and at once. Do *not* let this situation go on until a disaster occurs and you are too ill to cope with it.

I would like to repeat everything I have ever said to you about going slow. Realize, and *never* forget, that what you have in your life to suffer *is* what God asks of you, and it is enough to convert the world, because it is *His Son's Passion* and it matters more and is more effective than anything you could invent or do to convert the world.

Take certain days and offer (in the morning) *all* that happens on them *for* your husband.

Above all, do slow down every way; don't ask to reach the hilltop in a hurry. Don't forget what hill it is—Calvary. Don't forget you are carrying Christ's cross, and never, never forget how *slowly Christ* had to go up the hill carrying His cross....

28TH OCTOBER, 1949

... Better than anything at all which I could possibly say to you would be for you to read Alfred Wilson's book, *Pardon and Peace*, which really does discuss all your worries and every possible worry about confession. I will get it and send it to you, unless you let me know you already have it.

But I can say one or two things based on my personal knowledge of you and on my own experience of the misery of scruples. I suffered from them once for a few months, at the age of nine, and so ill did they make me that I had the Last Sacraments and was at the point of death: actually I was cured by the Holy Viaticum. I have suffered very many things since, of all kinds, but none of them ever came near the suffering of those few months of "scruples." I tell you this because I want to impress on you the fact that I do really know how *awful* it is, and when I say, as I do, that a *drastic* remedy alone can help, I say it not out of hardness but because I realize that what one needs is not soft soap but a *cure*.

You are suffering from anxiety neurosis; scruples are sometimes a symptom of it. Of course, there are countless other forms of scruples, and reasons for them; but as you suffer from anxiety in other ways, I am *convinced* it is the cause of yours. Of course Satan makes use of the easiest way for himself.

I think you ought to follow the following drastic rule, but as I have only time now to state it briefly without explanation, I shall have to explain why in my next letter—but you can be sure all I put here is orthodox—some out of the book I spoke of (I believe you *have* it?).

(1) Do not try *not to feel guilty*. Accept the feeling of guilt as just and offer it in reparation for all sin.

(2) Pray to make a good confession, then do not *allow* yourself more than *two minutes* time to examine your conscience. Confess *only* what comes to mind in that two minutes.

(3) *Never* repeat or go back on a confession. All you forget or are unsure of is forgiven anyway: you are *not* obliged to confess any but mortal sin. So long as you confess *something*, the rest is forgiven with it.

It is an insult to God to suppose He is trying to trip you up—sort of waiting for you to misstate something or forget something, and then, chuckling like a demon, say, "Ha, ha, she has done for herself—got all muddled up in the meat pie and damned herself!"

(4) Remember Confession, like Communion, is *first of all* a contact, a loving embrace with Our Lord. All He asks is that you should want to be sorry, because you want to come back closer than ever to Him. It does not depend on an exact recitation of sins but on a loving will to come closer to Him.

(5) After confession—say penance, at once, and *only once*—never mind how distracted. Repetitions of a penance don't count anyway.

(6) Just remind yourself of the conditions required for mortal sin. (a) Grave matter (in case of Friday abstinence, a sardine is not the grave matter, but *deliberate, wilful* defiance of the Church's authority). (b) Full knowledge—i.e. of the gravity, and that you are doing it—that it *is* grave sin. (c) Full consent. This implies deliberation; the will must be in condition for full consent, i.e. not coerced, unduly influenced, not a sin of weakness, or committed when drunk (getting drunk, if deliberate, could be grave sin, but not what is done after, in the fullest sense).

Now do follow these rules. Prayer: "Let me make a good confession."
Act of *sorrow*.
Two minutes' *only* soul search!
No going back on *any* of it.
Once you've made the confession—finis: ahead, closer love of God—all the rest *behind* you. Don't turn back from God to sort out an abandoned dung heap.

And—never stay away from Communion. You will never be, never could be, in *any* doubt about mortal sin. If there is doubt there is *no* mortal sin. That is certain.

All this sounds hard, but I know it's a certain cure....

9TH NOVEMBER, 1949

Now about your anxiety neurosis, etc. Be *certain* the devil will renew his attack, and be prepared for it.

Anxiety or any other nerves are not *cured* by the sacraments or by religion, though of course they are often helped by them, and if God chooses to work a miracle they could be. But it is one of the most frequent delusions of converts that once they are "in" the Church they will simply drop off the psychological habits of years. But no: the sacraments and the Church do something better than that; they enable one to suffer one's nerves, etc., and to give them an honourable place in one's life, to see what the meaning of them is. For neurosis is a tremendous, redeeming suffering. Its place in the Christ-life is Gethsemane.

I think that on the natural plane the first thing to do, for one's own peace of mind, is to *accept* one's suffering and fear and stop trying to escape from it.

You asked me how I managed to accept fear in the raids. I've just remembered (because it's the same sort of thing) that I never answered you. Well—perfectly simply. Instead of kidding myself and trying to minimize the danger or to find some distraction from it, I said to myself: "For as long as this raid lasts—an hour—or eight hours—you are going to be terrified. So are lots of people who don't deserve it as you do, so you must just carry on and be terrified, that's all"—and at once the *strain* ceased. Oh yes, I was terrified: I've often had to resort to sheer force to hide the fact that my teeth were chattering, and been unable to speak as my mouth was too dried up and stiff from funk. But at the same time I felt that God had put His hand right down through all the well upon well of darkness and horror between Him and me and was holding the central point of my soul; and I knew that *however* afraid I was then, it would not, even could not, break me. I always volunteered (after this discovery) for *most* frightful things (if called on to do so only!)—like Mobile First Aid in the street, and fire watching on the roof of Nell Gwynn: and always knew God was there in a special way, to accept the offering of fear. It's only when we try *not* to experience our special suffering that it can really break us.

As regards *fearful* worry—the obsessional sort that has suspense in it—like someone very dear, very ill—I find the rosary is of huge help. Even just holding it helps, and the most mechanical recitation of the prayers. It somehow gives one the sense of real contact with God, when one can't get it from any words or acts of one's own and yet cannot bear to be passive.

And you know, if you *can* relax, that does help—even toothache. I learnt this as a child from a saintly doctor we had. I had a very long, very painful illness, and he spent hours literally training me to loosen up every muscle and not to stiffen up and try to resist pain, either physically or mentally—with the result that the pain—*and fatigue*—were greatly reduced. I've tried relaxing every nerve and muscle in the dentist's chair, and found the stopping of teeth helped beyond belief by it.

If I were you I should not worry with de Caussade and his ilk. Most books of that sort are written by and for religious (monks and nuns), and once they have made a clean break from their family and the world, they have not got the same *kind* of troubles that we have. It is much easier to be "abandoned" when you are not tied up and twisted and rooted into those you love; and if you are a married woman with a family, you *must* love your family and you *must* mind what happens, and whether you can pay the rent, and whether there is anything in the larder, and so on. Your sanctity comes from putting your trust in God for yourself *and* your family, and you are not expected (by God) to be indifferent to those whom He has given to you to be loved by you! If you try to apply (as so many do) ideas which even in a monastery are difficult to practice, to life in the world, it will end in depression.

It's *not* wrong to worry or fear, but it is wrong not to accept worry and fear if they are your personal cross. Only hand out the worry and fear to Our Lord; ask Him to bear it with you.

I think the very best form of prayer for you is to rest. Fatigue is a main cause of neurosis, of over-sensitivity of conscience, and the arch-enemy of real trust in God. I know you are overwhelmed by work, but in general try to tackle nerves and worry in a large general way, through physical means: rest in all the ways you can. Do things, deliberately, a little more slowly; when you can sit down and take a little sleep, even for *three minutes*, do so. At Mass, do not try to pray; just try to put all you can into making the sign of the cross, sitting and kneeling, etc. Leave the *talking*, or, if He wills, the silence, to God. Try to go to bed a little earlier when most busy and most tired, and if worried or sleepless, say, or hold, the rosary in bed....

28TH DECEMBER, 1949

... I would go to Holy Communion as often as possible if I were you, but without making it a matter of "ought." If you are very restless at night, take a warm drink and don't worry, but when you can go without it, go to Holy Communion. God understands our weakness and knows our desires: just trust His love. Once this nervous tension is really eased, you will begin to sleep better and to find everything getting easier, but don't worry it into a nervous obsession. Ignore Satan—he hates it!

LONDON
8TH MARCH, 1950

I owe you abject apologies for not having answered your last letter, but I am glad to see that your troubles about faith seem to have cleared up.

I think that, should they return, you have only to remind yourself that faith *is* faith; it is not realization or knowledge. No *one* can realize what heaven is like, and no one is meant to be able to. The whole point of our life here is that we do live by faith, we *are* afraid of death, we are incapable of realizing eternal things, but we trust God and believe what He has told us.…

[Blessed Martin de Porres] cured a friend of mine who had been ill for months, and seemed to be in a sort of decline, completely worn out, with an exhausted heart, chronic bronchitis, and so on. She did not respond to the doctor's treatment at all, and having had *six months'* sick leave and got worse all through it, she decided that she must either be cured by a miracle, or give up her job for good. So she made the novena to Blessed Martin, and on the ninth day returned to work, perfectly well, her heart sound and normal, no cough, no fatigue, and to her chagrin she has been steadily putting on weight since! (about four months).

Let me know if you make a novena to him and I will join in with you.

Now I must stop writing and go to sleep, as it is late; day and night are all one to me now† and this solitude is lovely. All I really want is the Mass. But I have the Oratory in sight from my window, hear the Angelus and the Sanctus bell, and somehow seem to be surrounded by the Real Presence all the time!

(UNDATED)

… Briefly, my news is: I am at home, as you see, but have to go daily

---

† At this time Caryll was in bed with pneumonia.

to the hospital (and have been doing so since I left it, about 2½ weeks ago) for deep X-ray treatment. This treatment, though necessary, and wonderfully interesting from the scientific point of view, is very trying. It makes one feel simply flat out—exhaustion hardly describes it: you feel unable to move, to read or write, to speak, and in my case (I am told reactions to it vary) any attempt to do anything usually results in sickness—which for me, vain as I am, is the final humiliation! ...

Thank you indeed for your prayers. I am quite sure they have been and are a great support and a really creative influence for me, because, quite apart from the fact that I am, all things considered, doing very well, I am quite at peace mentally, and every moment of the experience I have had has been a wonderful and beautiful revelation of Christ. However, I shall leave that for a future letter, as I still am having treatment, and still find it difficult to write more than a little.

TERRICK, NEAR AYLESBURY
17TH SEPTEMBER, 1952

I am really sorry to have left your letters unanswered for so long. I know that you do know that it is not because I am indifferent or unsympathetic about your troubles, but quite honestly I have been unable to get half the things done that I ought to. My letters waiting for answers are a positive shame.

I have, however, been praying for you. I find that nowadays I cannot sleep much, but all the same when in bed I am too tired to write (as I used always to do at night). So this makes it possible for me to spend some hours every night praying for my friends, and I think I have said a rosary for you...*every* night for the last two months—usually at 4 o'clock in the morning, an hour at which I always wake up, as certainly as if I had an alarm clock set for that time. I am really very glad indeed to hear at last a little good news, and shall go on praying continually for a series of miracles to make it all come right and stay right. I am quite sure that all your suffering and patience *is* working miracles: God is *quite* surely watching, measuring, even allowing, every pang, every moment of fatigue, anxiety and distress, and suddenly it will all be given back to you in full measure, but changed into joy. You must try never to forget that God would not allow…you…to suffer the least fraction that He did not know to be not merely the *best* way to your ultimate joy, but the essential condition of it, and the *only* way to it. Why some people have to go through so much, and others so little (or it seems so), we shall never know on earth, but without any doubt at all it is all part of a plan of God's infinite love for each one of us, and in some way connected with our interrelation with each other. In the next life we shall find that the answer to this mystery is also the fullest and most astonishing answer to the mysterious beatitude, "Blessed are those that mourn, for they shall be comforted.…"

24TH OCTOBER, 1952

… About your question on suffering: I don't think you need to reproach yourself about your "acceptance" of it. First of all, this is a matter of the will; naturally you could not possibly *feel* glad to suffer—if you could, it would not be suffering at all. I rather think that this fact is at the root of a lot of our worries and anxieties about suffering. We read a lot of stuff about the saints "rejoicing in suffering," and stupidly (though naturally) imagine from this that they actually *enjoyed* suffering! There are, of course, people who in a queer perverted way *do* enjoy suffering, but they are not saints!

The acceptance of the saints must, of course, be the same as Our Lord's acceptance of His Passion—something before which He shrank and of which He felt every faintest quiver. If anyone who had to suffer became insensitive and did not feel it, but instead felt a certain smugness in their own ability to suffer, it really would be utterly useless—it would not really be suffering at all.

Very well, it's no use hoping to *enjoy* what we have to suffer, or even that we may have a feeling of accomplishment or some such thing:

everything in human nature, if our suffering really *is* suffering, must smart and agonize under it, and we must confess with Our Lord that it is something wholly and absolutely against our will.

I am afraid in the first place the acceptance has to be a sheer *act of will*. It is true, as you say, that I did suffer enough…to understand a little of what you feel, although I know I did not go through anything approaching your grief. I suppose we each have to take the measure of our capacity and no more, since more we *can't* take.…

I'm afraid there is no short cut, and no hope of suffering without *feeling* it. The only thing to do, so far as *I* know, is to go on and on repeating this prayer, even if it seems to be a mechanical repetition—"Lord, into Thy hands"—and then say, "I confide X, or myself"—and perhaps it can help to meditate on what you mean by "into Thy hands"—hands of infinite tenderness, infinite love, absolute power.

There is another thing I have had to learn—and still need to learn far more deeply and lastingly—namely, not to foster bitterness, resentment and dislike.… This I have found very hard, but I have realized for very long that so long as these feelings were fermenting in me, I could hardly expect God to answer my prayers.

About that, as about all the rest of it, I made a novena to Blessed Martin de Porres, a most amazing saint, who seems to answer prayers quite irrespectively of how wicked or "unworthy" one is. It is that which encourages me to pray to him, and his answers are truly miraculous.

I well understand your anxiety about health and about your eyes, for I have both. I have been to an oculist, recommended to me and supposed to be very good, but the new glasses he gave me are useless: I now have to *feel*, not look, at my carving tools to see if they are the right way up! Your knitting is, as you say, useful, but it is very much more than useful, it is absolutely beautiful. It is indeed sad that you can't do any more of that wonderful fine work you used to do, but your knitting really is an art in itself, and one that must bring a lot of comfort and joy to many people.

About your health. If the doctor can't diagnose what is or is not wrong with you, why not go to the hospital and have a thorough examination, including X-rays?

Of course I know, all too well, what a fearful trial this is, and how embarrassing, but at least, if you could *make* yourself face it, it would result either in finding out without any delay or uncertainty what *is* wrong, and putting it right in good time, or else in finding that it is nothing very serious, and so getting relief of mind. I really would advise you to take this course.

Personally I regard having to go to the hospital for examinations as an earthly purgatory, in spite of the wonderful contacts one has there with people who suffer more than I ever have, and with heroism. But all the same I realize how simply marvellous the modern methods of research and cure are, and that there is little left now that they can't overcome.

I have to go every three months; I hate it, but at the same time I am grateful. Last time I went, last Tuesday, things were not so good as usual, with the result that I have to go again next Monday, *and* next Tuesday, to get the results of X-rays and blood tests. Please say a prayer for me. I think it will be O.K., and I marvel at the trouble and care they take.

I was interested in your lecture on Margaret Clitheroe—I wish I could have heard it. Why not pray to her to help you? I expect you do!

(UNDATED)

… About the rosary—this of course applies to prayer generally—*most certainly* it is not a good thing from any point of view to gabble prayers: far better to let not only one decade of the rosary but even one Our Father or one Hail Mary take you a week to say. Prayer *should* be a deep inner rest, something which calms you and increases your trust (the more it *does* increase your trust, the more it gives you inner peace and rest).

In a busy and harassed life this *could* not be the result of prayer, if the most important thing were how many words you can get said in a day! Lots of deeply holy and prayerful people *can't* say *one*, even at Mass. Prayer, as the Catechism tells us, is "raising the heart and mind to God"—there need be no words, but only an inexpressible adherence to God, an attitude of mind and heart, a simple wordless desire to be one with Him. This makes it inevitable that one recognizes His will for one at the moment in every circumstance, and knows that every act, however trivial, done in this spirit, is done for His glory and *is* prayer.

Personally I find the best way is that used by the Russian *starets* (holy man) and also by St. Ignatius—simply saying (not necessarily with the lips) the name of Jesus, or the word "God," as often as you can, until it is woven all through the day, and this prayer can be further simplified by simply "*breathing*" it (the name of Jesus, or God, or whatever you like)—that is "saying" or "thinking" it in your mind with every breath you draw in.

If even this seems a strain, it is enough to offer all your thoughts, words and acts to God in the morning, and leave it at that.

The rosary in particular—well, the reason it is being strongly urged as a devotion now is because, in all her apparitions, or most of them, Our Lady herself has asked us to use it. The forms of prayer I have spoken of are to some extent contemplative, and by no means everyone has even a little gift of contemplation; many good people find it is only by *saying* prayers that they can pray at all, and when it comes to praying *together*, as a family or a congregation, the repetition becomes a necessity; you couldn't stop while each person made his own pace and his individual meditation during the rosary, but it is certain that thousands who gather together to say it would not otherwise pray at all—and each of them is encouraged to meditate *when* alone, and so on....

Terrick, near Aylesbury
14th October, 1953

... Your final question is: "How not worry?"!

Well, if only I had an answer to meet that, how gladly I would give it to you, and apply it to myself! But of course there is no short cut to not worrying.

It does not necessarily imply want of trust; in fact, it may be that what God asks of you is to accept it, and not to worry about worrying!

Trust does not, of course, mean that you trust God to remove the causes of worry, though if you persevere in prayer in spite of all setbacks, He may do that; but trust really means that, however impossible it is to realize this emotionally, your *will* accepts as a certainty that *whatever* God allows to happen *is*, in His plan of love, what is *really* best for you and those whom you love.

"Surrender" to God's will does not of course mean being able to *want* disaster!

It does mean believing, blindly of course, that whatever happens, and whatever you *feel* about it, you *are* in His hands, and so are those you love.

The more you say, "I must not worry," the more you will: I think it better simply to offer the worrying to God.…

I have the temperament which just has to face the worst possibility, and I think, when one does, one realizes that the very worst *can* be accepted. My way is to say in every emergency, "Now what is the worst that *can* happen?", and then, "So wot?" That works with me—but not with everyone. One friend of mine believes firmly in putting her head in the sand and refuses to face things, even when they actually happen—and she certainly does get through things apparently without a scar, though she has had things to suffer that would shatter most other people.

One important point is the physical side. If one is tired or run down, ill in any way, it is much more difficult to attain serenity. Nerves torment one, and worry goes with them. Your troubles are enough to tire you, but I do think the new home will help, by reducing the work and the financial strain.…

17TH FEBRUARY, 1954

I am terribly ashamed because I have not written before and answered your last letter.

But first of all, thank you very much indeed for your very generous subscription to the Loaves and Fishes. It is so wonderful when somebody sends a subscription without having had a written reminder (and also so rare!). You ask how the Loaves and Fishes are doing. They are doing moderately well, but as I know to my shame, not nearly so well as they could do if I put more energy into the work myself. To run the thing properly it requires someone who really cares about it, and who has the time and other means to make it their whole-time job; I *do* really care about it very much, but I already have more than one whole-time job and can't do all I should. However, a good deal has been done this year, and it is a miracle how the thing survives and goes on living. The chief thing has been getting jobs for "Sea-horses"—very often ones whom, one would think, it would be impossible to get a job for, either because they are too old, or temperamentally too difficult. "Sea-horses," you know, are very often people who are always on the lookout for slights, fearfully self-deluded, and almost impossible to get on with. They are often most unwilling to make themselves pleasant or adjust themselves in any way to other people or to circumstances. They often live in a world of unreality. This makes it extremely difficult to get jobs for them, and one more or less has to rely on the very rare employers who are charitable enough to humour them.

    I do not know of a book wholly on the subject of hope, though if there was one it would certainly do a world of good. But oddly enough I came across something the other day in an American periodical which I thought a wonderful idea. It was an answer to a question sent in by a reader who said that she had been deserted by her husband and could not pray without bitterness (or something like that). The answer was to pray in the words of the psalms, and I really do think that that is worth considering.

    When one becomes overwhelmed by one's personal troubles, plus weariness, probably plus the loneliness of having no one near at hand to whom one can talk, and who will understand if one does, it becomes very difficult indeed to say, or to mean, "one's own" prayers; but in the psalms one does find every possible human experience, and even to read them seems to be putting oneself in touch with someone who has experienced *all* our own feelings.

I will send you the copy of the magazine with this in it, also two other copies, because as well as this very good bit of advice they contain some meditations of my own on the Stations of the Cross, which might interest you, though I do not think much of them myself! ...

> *The above letter was written within the last few months of Caryll's life. Her* Stations of the Cross *was published later in book form and helped many people—at the time she made the meditations she was walking the road of the Cross herself. In a state of constant pain and exhaustion ("she suffered greatly," her doctor told me, "and uncomplainingly"), she was still carrying on a work started in youth—the* Loaves and Fishes. *Begun in the early 1930s, before the Welfare State existed, it was designed to help those who even in a Welfare State go unassisted—the helpless poor whom no law helps or who know not the law that might help them, the secret poor who hide their poverty, who are, in St. Vincent's phrase, "pauvres honteux." These especially were christened "Sea-horses"; holding their heads high, they tend to rebuff help and must be tactfully approached by the "Sprats," as members of the Society were called. A very personal, secret work had been done by this small group for twenty years; Caryll was still doing it within months of her death. The operation was so conducted that when Sprats (themselves often on the edge of poverty) got money from wealthier friends, the Sea-horses never suspected it to be other than a personal gift from a friend—the Sprat who in fact knew them and could approach them with affectionate understanding.*

XII

To a Friend with a Nervous Illness

This young friend had several years' nervous illness following a disturbed childhood and adolescence. She has since been able to follow a calling in which she frequently remembers the confidence which Caryll always maintained in her, when no one else did so. This not only still helps her, but those in turn who now come to her for help: death did not destroy their friendship.

LONDON
23RD AUGUST, 1947

... The thing I do most seriously want to stress, although I don't think I really need to, as your letter suggests you are fully conscious of it, is that you should not let delays disturb you, but realize that you most definitely are already a member of the Church, and what you are waiting for so painfully is not the Faith, but the consolations of the Faith; so that you can certainly offer all this waiting and patience for other people—for those who have no faith, and who *will* get it, even if you never know of them in this life, because *you* have paid the price for them. Also you can do a most lovely work of charity by offering up some of it for the souls in Purgatory who, having glimpsed God face to face, must now *wait* for His presence, or for their awareness of it, for *their* presence with Him....

It is a most blessed thing in you, that instead of becoming *obsessed* by your own soul as so many do, your worries are about others, and you put the beautiful holiness of charity and love before the excessive preoccupation with personal perfection, which, though I suppose I should not say it, destroys so many souls in my eyes.

Of course, I don't mean one should not try to be good, but only that one should try it first of all through love of others, as you evidently do.

But we have to love our neighbour "as ourself," so presumably must "love ourself," which would mean, love to be the self God wants us to be; and, for that end and within that limit, a certain amount of what *looks* like selfishness is self-defence, in the sense that it is a form of self-defence to eat bread. *Some* help and strength of a supernatural sort is your necessity; your soul needs it as imperatively as your body needs food, and it would be wrong to deny it to yourself....

Now about a spiritual Communion daily. I did not mean you to read through the Mass prayers daily; it is not necessary to do that even *at* Mass. A spiritual Communion can be made by a single simple, loving desire to receive Our Lord in the Blessed Sacrament, an act in your own words telling Him that you long to receive Him in the Blessed Sacrament and asking Him at all events not to delay coming to your soul, and to come now.

No more is necessary; *less* is enough—an unformulated, wordless desire on which for a *moment* you pause, giving your will to it, is enough.

If, however, you *have* time and want to do more, you can (and this is also a perfectly good method of actually taking part in the Mass) make four simple acts (prayers in your own words), corresponding to the four great motives of the Mass.

First, Contrition—an act of contrition which corresponds to the Confiteor and Kyrie Eleison, and can be as short and simple as "My God, I am sorry for all my sins; please forgive me."

Second, Praise and Faith, a joyful profession of faith on a note of joy *because* of the wonder of it. This corresponds to the Gloria and the Gospel and Creed, and can be as simple as "I believe in the teaching of the Church because it is *your* teaching. I praise, adore and thank you for our faith."

Third, Offering—and this is the Offertory, the offering up of the bread and wine to be consecrated: "I offer myself, today, as I am—my temptations, failures, triumphs, what I shall do, say, think, suffer, enjoy: all to be changed into Christ."

And, finally, the Communion: "Come to me, Jesus Christ, food of my soul."

Four such simple, brief acts, in your own words, are a spiritual Mass and Communion, and afterwards you can go to your day, to your father, mother, sister, friends, dogs, with Christ's love in your heart, and He will act in you and for you.

These are clumsy enough and crude suggestions—you need not follow them. I hope you will soon have some good, understanding priest to instruct you, to whom you can turn for far more definite and dependable as well as wiser advice than I can give to you, but in the meantime, if it is any help at all to you to write more to me, or to discuss any other difficulties, I am here, at your service and only most eager to answer you to the best of my ability....

London
30th April, 1948

... About your own trials—first, that of the war within you, for and against striving for perfection:

I know that you can't help feeling that conflict, but I believe the only solution is to concentrate absolutely on God, especially on Christ in your own soul—not even looking to see how *you* are getting on, only looking to see if He is getting stronger in you. I learnt a lot that way from Clare. If you concentrate on the spark of Christ-life in your soul—the Infant Christ, in you—as one has to concentrate on keeping the little flame of life burning in a frail little infant, I think you would find that day after day *everything* is given to Christ quite naturally and easily, and you hardly noticing it.…

I feel sure that God is only concerned with the simple fact of your *love* for Him, not with a lot of details of your perfection. I often think that the ideal of our perfection that we set up and often go through torture to achieve, may not be *God's* idea of how He wants us to be at all. That may be something quite different that we never would have thought of, and what seems like a failure to us may really be something bringing us closer to *His* plan for us—so we shouldn't grieve. The only thing to do, I think, is to keep making short little interior acts of love, asking God to fashion us to His own design; then He certainly will, and sooner or later we certainly will be just what He wants us to be.

But I only tell you my own way; yours may be different, and if it is, it is certainly the best way for *you*.

I think that Confession must be a very real trial to anyone as sensitive as you are. No one likes it; the toughest old Catholics of my acquaintance get a sort of squiggle in their inside over even the most paltry recitation of their sins, and nearly all have been through searching periods of nervous scruples which leave a miserable association of ideas.

A few basic facts can help:

(1) It isn't really confession, it is *penance*: the confession is only part of the sacrament, not the chief part. What matters is sorrow for sin.

(2) Sorrow for sin is just the *will to be sorry*, proved by receiving the sacrament of penance. It is not a feeling that we *are* sorry.

(3) This ought to be 1, not 3. Penance is a form of Communion, a means of union with Christ—that, before all else.

(4) All the essential is done by God, on His side. He doesn't do it to trip us up—I mean He is there with open arms to take us to His heart, and He makes it as easy as possible for us to come. He isn't there rubbing His hands and saying, "Ha! X forgot something! I'll jump on her for that!"

(5) What you do forget is forgiven.…

(6) You *need* only confess mortal sin. You need not confess *any* venial sins. All you must do to be absolved is to confess *a* [venial] sin, not all—all are included in the forgiveness. Sometimes scrupulous people are well advised only to confess one sin.

(7) To imagine, once you've done your best, that God isn't satisfied, is an insult to God. He is overjoyed, and so should you be.

I am sure—and I can see it in your letter, too—that since you became a Catholic you are growing in the supernatural life enormously, and will go on and on getting more and more one with God, in will and heart and mind.

LONDON
27TH JULY, 1948

... I have prayed now to be allowed not to give you wrong advice, for you are much holier than I am, and certainly much wiser and more thoughtful than I was at your age, and I am not in any way qualified to guide you; so take everything I say always simply as the words of a friend, to be weighed for what they are worth and disregarded if they seem not to be helpful.

About confession, have you got a book called *Pardon and Peace*, by Alfred Wilson, C.P.? If not, do get it and read it and go on reading it, and if you *have* read it, read it again. It answers all your questions, and not only that, any others you could possibly think of about confession, and it helps you to know how, when, how much, how often to examine your conscience. The author, who must be a magnificently understanding priest, addresses himself separately to every type of person—the oversensitive, sensitive, scrupulous, the hardened—and has a really effective prescription for them all. He stresses, all through all of what he says, that the one great central idea to concentrate on in confession is Gods tremendous love and mercy for us, and he tells you how to go about curing the sort of anxiety and worry over your confession which is, though unconsciously, a sort of denial of it (of God's love).

We are so apt to forget that it is Christ who does the most important things in the sacrament, and what He asks of us, to make Him able to do His part, is a very small minimum. I think this priest would advise you personally to give only three minutes *at the outside* to the examination of conscience, but be sure to pray briefly and lovingly for the grace to make a good confession before you start. If you do that, you can safely trust it to God. You are not bound to confess venial sins *at all*, even if you remember them at the time, and you are almost bound—in fact, really bound—not to work up and magnify imperfections "to be on the safe side." Anyway, that would not make you safe—far from it. It would blind you to God's loving desire to forgive you and take you closer to His heart. Only one thing ever makes you safe—putting your trust in God.

I should say, never omit your regular confession without some real reason (not being able to go out, or something). But never worry over it either. If you have some deliberate sin in your past life, confess that (mention what it is) and tell God that you are sorry for all the sins of your whole life, remembered and forgotten. That's all that's needed, and it's that which will bring you closer to God every time.

I shall write again in detail about your other query, but briefly, my answer is this. Aim at your highest; don't dream of aiming at mediocracy[†]; don't be put off by those who tell you sanctity is dangerous. But don't let the concentration be on self or on planned mortification. Just try to act in every moment as it arises as Our Lord would have done, and read the Gospel often, for you will see that Our Lord, though very austere in His life, was not strained or fanatic. *He* entered into His friends' pleasures and had many human wishes, even asking for human sympathy and being grateful and delighted by natural expressions of love shown to Him. Our Lord put *love* first; His austerity was a natural expression of love.

Don't fetter your soul with self-made rules and resolutions. Put your faith in God; ask Him to work *His* will in you, and then just turn

---

" Mediocracy": a community ruled by the mediocre.

your eyes on *Him*. You will then do as He wants without any strain, and happily. But more of this later—I must catch the post....

LONDON
20TH JANUARY, 1950

I haven't your letter in front of me, as Clare is asleep (my chance to write at all!) and I am afraid of waking her if I open the cupboard door to get it. From this you can judge that Clare is again staying with me. However, I read your letter many times and prayed about it, and so I will give you such advice as I can (but you must make allowances if I do not remember perfectly all that you say, though I think I do).

The main point is about going to Holy Communion without feeling.

I say, without any hesitation, go as often as you can, daily if possible, with or *without* feeling. Do not let what *you* feel have any sort of influence on you at all; even if you feel that you are utterly *unfit to go* to Holy Communion, ignore it and go just the same. If, however, you are very tired or physically ill, so that it would be a real effort and strain to get up before your day's work to go to Mass, on a weekday, then accept your limitations humbly, and on that day sleep a little longer and offer your weakness to God.

About Holy Communion. Our mistake is that we think of it too much from *our* side. If we can only realize that it is much more Our *Lord's Communion with us*, than ours with Him, we would never hesitate to go. It is not what we *feel* that matters, but what He *wants*.

Think how touching His words are when, at the Last Supper, He says: "With desire have I desired to eat this Pasch with you." In other words (and they are addressed to you personally, every time you go to Holy Communion), "I have longed and longed to come to this Communion with *you*." The fact is, Our Lord has waited two thousand years in the Host for *you*, and He longs for every Communion you make. Feeling can be a very good thing and a great help, but love is essentially an act of will, and it is in fact a *greater act of love* to go to Holy Communion without feeling, as dry as dust and wrestling with distractions, than it is to go in raptures! You go, not because you want to go, but because Christ wants to come to you. That is the thing that really matters.

But I do warn you not to strain your body; go to early Mass when you can do so without undue fatigue, but remember, the fact that you are not strong is allowed by God, and is something for you to offer up to Him and so to use for His glory. To try to tax your physical strength too much would be wrong....

London
20th March, 1950

… I am praying for you every day, but much more asking Our Lord Himself to pray to His Father for you. Or I suppose I should say, using His power and love to pray for you with. I am also asking Our Lady and all the angels and saints to pray for you, and I know that *they* will be round you in a tremendous strength of compassion and love.

You have no need to look round for mortifications for Lent, and I do hope and pray that Easter will be a real Easter for you, a Resurrection full of the loveliness and joy and new flowering of the life that is the Light of the world. I expect that you love that Easter morning cry of "Lumen Christi" as much as I do. May it sing out joyfully in your own heart....

Terrick, near Aylesbury
28th May, 1952

I do indeed feel sorry that again you have to stay in bed in this lovely weather, but perhaps it will not be for so long as you expect, and you will be able to get up and enjoy the sun while it is still shining.

When will you be twenty-one? I shall pray every day that you will then be well enough to enjoy your birthday, and will go on getting better and better.

I am glad you are reading *The Cloud of Unknowing*. It is one of my favourite books. The only one that I like equally is *Revelations of Divine Love* by Blessed Juliana of Norwich. Goodier seems to me one of the *most* human and comforting of authors—I knew him, and thought him a deeply holy person.

I was most interested about Littleton Powys. The only book I have read (so far) of Elizabeth Myers is her letters, but that made me long to read every word that she has ever written; and as soon as I possibly can, I shall....

I agree with you about the "importance of living." I go further; it seems to me that the very great thing is to be able to *enjoy* life. When I was in the hospital last year and they told me, as they did, that they were not at all sure that they could operate, I felt no fear of death, though I did not *want* to die, as I knew how lonely it would leave my friend, with whom I have lived for twenty-eight years. But what I *did* feel was remorse, because I realized that I had never really *let* myself *enjoy* life—so many scruples and inhibitions and things preventing me from really enjoying the sheer loveliness of the world, the people in it, and even the material things in it—food, drink, the sun, spending money, etc. I imagine that will sound very low to you. But when my poor old mother died, in 1950, in St. Georges Hospital, I went out into the Park, opposite the hospital, and sat down and suddenly realized how *lovely* it was—the sky, the bare trees (it was November), the grass, the very touch of the air—and it suddenly swept over me, with a terrible pang, that my old mother had never really *enjoyed* life. She was always worried, always working, always thinking about money—never, or certainly hardly ever, sufficiently *detached from self* to enjoy the beauties and pleasures of this life. Then and there I made up my mind to enjoy my own, at the expense of my own vanity, self-love, anxiety (another form of self-love), and everything else. When, following hard on this, I nearly lost my own life, I made only one resolution: if I was given another chance (as I have been), I would *enjoy* everything in life that I can, for as long as I can, and as wholly as I can.

I hope your budgie is a great success; we have had them in our time, and ours were very tame, walking about the room, on our shoulders, etc. But I find it difficult to like birds as pets.

I have really loved one, though—a bullfinch I had when I was a child, who became like a dog; he went everywhere with me, sitting on my shoulder or in my pocket, out for walks, to the kindergarten school and everywhere, and at night he slept on my pillow.

Clare has made the "Normous Kiss" for you which I enclose, and I guided her hand to write the "letter." She asked herself to write to you when I told her I was doing so.

9TH JUNE, 1952

Thank you very much indeed for your letter; it makes it very much easier for me to understand your difficulties. But as a matter of fact, I think I do understand, in so far as any human being can ever understand another, because some of them I have lived through myself....

I know that you act, very often, under a kind of compulsion, and your sudden flights and spontaneous acts probably mean that you fear you will be unable to achieve your end at all if you delay. But actually you *could*, every time, and without making misunderstanding and difficulties for yourself....

However, in view of what I am about to say, I am being very foolish in dwelling on any of this, because what I *am* about to say is: if you sincerely wish to be well and to do something worth while with your life, the *first* step towards it is absolutely to refuse to dwell on the past. What is past *is* past; it cannot be undone, it cannot be changed by self-torture. When it is sinful it can be and should be confessed once, and *only* once, and then forgotten; when it is just a mistaken, confused or foolish thing, it should simply be left alone.

What provokes this little outburst from me is your remark: "I cannot defend myself at all and blame myself and always will do."

DON'T!—forget it!

Fairly lately I visited a *very* dear aunt of mine. We love each other deeply, but have quite opposite temperaments. She is absorbed in her possessions, especially fabulously valuable antiques, and her flat is filled with such objects, especially things like old Chinese jade vases, etc. Well, I, wishing to be helpful, agreed to dust her room—even insisted—and the very first thing I did was to break her most precious and most beloved (by her) antique Chinese vase! Imagine my horror—there was no hope at all of mending it; it was just shattered into fragments.

My aunt took it marvellously, but I, of course, was simply devastated by remorse. Then she became angry. "Caryll," she said, "stop this nonsense at once. Nothing you feel will mend it; it's broken, let's forget it. What earthly good will it do for you to go around moaning and grieving all day? You are just going to *ruin* the little time we have together for both of us. What has happened, five minutes or five years ago, is *past*. For God's sake *let it be* past and forget it, if not for your own sake, for the sake of others."

I took that to heart, and saw not only what wisdom it contained but what courage and charity to carry it out—so *much* more than remorse—which, by the by, is always selfish.

17TH JULY

I am shocked to see that I started this letter over a week ago; I *have* tried to go on with it every day, but have *always* been interrupted. This really should teach me to begin letters with essentials, not inessentials as I have done this one.

Now to get to the essentials. I have been through much that you are going through. I also took to starving myself as a very young child, and later as an adolescent, and I too did it because I wanted to be ill. My reasons for wanting to be ill were involved, and too long a story to attempt here. But I have learnt from bitter experience what happens, and I can tell you one or two things about how to get well.

The great difficulty is that once you *have* starved to any real extent, your mind and your will become ill. I don't mean that you are mad, but that vitamin deficiency does affect the brain, which is the tool the will has to use. One knows, for example, that lack of certain vitamins impairs the sight, in some cases causing temporary blindness; it is the same cause. This means that, although you can see in theory that it is desirable to be well, and right to try to get well, and though you really want to *want* to be well, you are not physically fit enough to be able to want it with your whole self. You are now in greater conflict with yourself than before you got ill. At first your illness did provide you with an escape from what you feared, but now you are not only faced with the obligation of overcoming *that* fear, but of overcoming the illness too, and now, in the state of weakness that you are in, you have not got the capacity to form sound judgments or to control your impulses as you would have if you were well.

You say, "I don't think anything can cure me really except a desire to *do* something which can override the fear I have of the future."

Well, the point is, you are trying to be cured without really being cured at all. I mean, you wish to become driven by some *compulsion* stronger than your fear, in order, though you perhaps don't realize it, that you may be cured without making persistent efforts yourself. You simply want one compulsion to overcome another, while your poor little *will* is swept along like a dead leaf in a storm—and you want to *want* to do this "something." You do *not* want the effort involved in doing a number of things you *don't* want, in order to become fit in every way, physically and mentally, to do something worth while with your life.

We simply must face these hard facts; no matter how strong a desire you had to do something, that by itself could not and would not cure you now, and in the attempt to do it you would break down. Already this has happened more than once, and each time you have resorted to flight. The reason is this: you are trying on these occasions to overcome the whole—to you—terrific bogey by what is indeed an act of will in one sense, but is the act of a will that is sick and quite unable in its weak (physically) state to cope with *any* of the initial difficulties, all of which have the aspect of fear for you.

You are simply trying to overcome your fears by doing violence to yourself, and you are not strong enough to stand that violence.

Now, a *real* act of will, from which you could start innumerable acts of will which *could* ultimately cure you, would be to determine to do those things you do *not* want to, day by day, as they arise, to get your body fit.

It is as useless to look to the future now as it is to look morbidly at the past. Every time you try to face the future, to see *beyond* the duration of your illness, your inevitable reaction is to try to somehow muster enough violence in yourself to oppose the bogey. In plain words, you are opposing violence with violence—and it can only be destructive to you to do that.

You must start by small, gentle acts of will; nurse your will, give it small tasks but let it be set in the right direction.

Useless to say, "Now I will be perfectly normal and fit and I will want to be." But useful and creative to say, "I will drink this glass of milk, and so be a tiny bit stronger this morning."

Very *gradually* you will build up enough strength of mind and body by these *little* acts of will to *really* want to get well. But it *must* be gradual. I think too that you should only attempt a moderate diet, not stuffing. You can increase what you eat very gradually, and as your appetite and your will to be well increase too—as they will do.

Now, if you will begin to make such acts of will, every single thing you do will be a prayer, a prayer which is so rooted in Our Lord's prayer, "Not my will but thine be done!", that it will have immense power as reparation for all the world's sin, and through your very conflict, illness and disability, you will be doing something terrific towards redeeming the world.

The fact that at various times there may have been some fault on your part which has helped to induce your illness does not in the least take away from the extraordinary power it could be to you now, in co-operation with Christ in His work of redemption.

Yes, let every meal be a prayer, every hour of sleep, every denial of an impulse to overdo brings you feel a compulsion to—and believe me, you will at one and the same time cure yourself and cure the sufferings of the world.

You see, *God's* will for you is to serve Him, in His way, as He chooses, *now*. It is only a want of humility to think of extreme vocations, like being a nun or a nurse, while you try to bypass your present obvious vocation, which is to restore your will to God's, so that you may become what *He* wants you to be, and may be able to use the faculties He has given to you for His service. *Today* you have to use what you have today, and do not look beyond it. You have your suffering of mind and body, you have that hardest of all things, the building up of your will by doing what you don't, and at present *can't*, feel you want to.

You know a person in a very weak state physically is not *able* to imagine how they would feel and what they would want if they felt well—they have not got the capacity to enjoy anything that a state of wellbeing gives them, and it is no use trying to imagine oneself feeling what one can't. One can only discipline oneself gradually to do those things which will repair their faculty for joy in life.

You ask me if I think you should go to a home. Well, I did recommend the one at Stroud which is not, and is not like, a nursing home, but where I feel sure it would be made easier for you to build up your will.

You see, you *need* to obey to achieve this, to let someone else make decisions and map out your daily life for you; in obedience you not only get the humility which floods your soul with grace, but you also get the emotional and psychological rest which is essential to you.

The circumstances at home result in continual inner conflict. Obviously there is tension *all* the time. Your mother's very love for you makes her anxious all the time, and there can only be a feeling of conflict as an undercurrent even to your more harmonious days.

This spells unrest all the time—even when you are asleep—and also, though you don't yet see it, you are literally holding on with both hands to your *fear* of being away from your mother.

If you would go away for one month and stay away, and obey those in care of you, you would *lose* that fear.

Do write again and let me know all you can and will about yourself. Another thing. It has come home to me so strongly lately how *much* little Catholic children need a book of *really* beautiful pictures of Our Lord. I remember all the stories I loved as a child because of the pictures. The other day the priest at Prince's Risborough said the same, and he said, "If only Edmond Dulac had done pictures of the life of Christ!"

I search in vain for books to keep Clare quiet at Mass—but as she can't read, and the pictures are so slight and poor, nothing works. In fact, I am determined to try to get time to make her one myself, big coloured pictures, full of the details that children love, and done in the conventional forms I *don't* like using. In fact, as close as I can to a crib of Edmond Dulac. The pictures must tell everything, so that no text at all is required.

Unhappily, such a picture book would cost a fortune to publish, and I'm afraid that is one reason why there is not one available. But another reason is that no illustrator seems to think the story of Christ worth doing beautifully.

Perhaps if you did it, and you could, a publisher *would* take it, but if not it could still bring the first and most lasting impression of God to countless little children, and perhaps you could have an exhibition of it. Think it over....

LONDON
11TH JANUARY, 1953

... I am terribly sorry to hear about all the unhappiness and disturbances which you had at Christmas time, but I see that in spite of it you are fighting a *winning* battle, and magnificently, and it is my belief that this year will see you well! ...

Now I want to answer the things you ask me to in your letter, before saying anything else, because I won't have time to write long and may be interrupted at any moment, and I think that nothing is so maddening as to get an "answer" to a letter which is in fact not an answer at all.

You say, "I cannot pray, or concentrate, or paint" (when you are upset). Well now, it may be, and I am sure is true that you cannot at those times concentrate or paint: then you say, "Should I try to pray much, or have just a few short times in the day?"

You should "pray without ceasing"—but, not verbal prayer, not mental prayer, but the prayer of the body, and the prayer of acceptance and immolation. *Say* only one prayer a day; the morning offering of the Apostolate of Prayer is ideal: "O my God, I offer you all my words, thoughts, actions and sufferings today, in union with your divine heart in the Holy Mass." Then let your prayer be simply your offering of yourself to do God's will, to *rest* and *relax* in Him, and to offer everything you *do* as a prayer; for example, if you have a little sleep, offer that; offer each mouthful of food that you eat, offer whatever you suffer, but all this simply and without any attempt at a formal offering in words, or any kind of meditation, or *thinking* about God.

Actually this kind of prayer that I propose to you brings you closer to God than anything you *can* say or *think* yourself, because it breaks down every barrier between you and God, every shred of resistance to His will, and allows *Him* to speak to *you*, to hold you in His hands and surround you with His love. You imagine God to be far away from you, but really He is so *close* that you can't see Him, like a child can't see her mother's face, if the mother is pressing her to her heart.

Now you ask how to spend the time to the best advantage mentally and physically as well as spiritually. As dressing dolls *does* absorb you, and I know how exquisitely you do it, I should certainly go on doing it. You might also interest yourself in making other toys, especially soft ones that you can sew, teddy bears, all sorts of cuddly animals, etc., especially with clothes to take on and off. I think all teddy bears need knitted suits! There is *endless* scope in toymaking, and besides being fascinating, it is lucrative. I have had several friends who made good incomes by it.

I would also advise you to make your own little indoor garden in your room, with a window box, and a few pots, or even a tub with a rose tree in it. I know a crippled person who can never go out who has got great joy this way. She has ivy plants, which she trains to grow (on sticks and things) in all sorts of fascinating ways, and a small rose tree, several baby cactuses (or should I say cacti?) and a window box, at present beginning to shine with pale crocuses. The thing is, that having growing things to look after gives one "something" that nothing else does.

I am delighted to hear about your American friend, and I hope that it will ripen more and more and bring you both joy; don't build too much on it, but put it into God's hands and go on writing. I shall pray that it may be your way to happiness....

TERRICK, NEAR AYLESBURY
22ND AUGUST, 1953

... I am delighted to hear such good news from you. Certainly it does sound lovely at X, and I thank God for bringing you somewhere there is such peace, and the sacraments given to you so easily. What a wonderful thing God's love is, always overflowing, always following you and, if one may say so, spoiling you—I am terribly glad for you that it is so.

Naturally you must have black days—God knows we all do!—but they will become more and more easy to accept, and to forget, as you gain in strength. Moreover, the more you do gain in strength, the more you will want to, and the happier you will be....

LONDON
31ST OCTOBER, 1953

... I am *very* sorry to hear of your breakdown, but at the same time I think that if it was the only thing to stop you from sacrificing your very great creative gifts to nursing and ward-maiding, then it is something to be thankful for.

You are right, God gives one talents to *use*, not to crush—remember the parable of the talents? To have an art at your finger tips and in your mind, as you have, is a trust; you are meant to develop and use it, partly because it is only by doing so that you can fully integrate your own personality—and that is another way of saying "save your soul"—and partly because you must give to the world, to the millions who are starved for beauty, the beauty that God has given into your trust for that purpose....

I always notice that Christ's whole attitude as a man, a *real* man, of course, was simply one of perfect acceptance: "I have come not to do my own will but the will of him who sent me": "Not my will, but thy will be done."

No doubt, one who loved men as He did would have longed to heal *all* their sickness, to enlighten *all* their minds, to transform the world by miracle upon miracle of love, but God did not will that for Him. On the contrary, He willed that He should be, humanly speaking, a failure, should be nailed to the cross and suffer there in helplessness. Indeed, the moment in which His love was consummated, in which the crisis of His redeeming power was reached, was when the hands that could heal with a touch were nailed back out of reach!

You made a really magnificent effort in doing that work in hospital, and when you do *anything* in sincere desire to serve God, not one gesture or word or thought is wasted—all the love you put into what you did will be with you for ever and ever, but clearly God is showing you that that is *not* your vocation. His will for you now is to be obedient and to do as the doctor tells you, and by so doing not only will you come to fulfil your real vocation, but you will work the miracle of curing the suffering and anxiety of your parents. I see by what you say about the expression on your face when people come in, that you realize far, far more than I can tell you the power given to you to love and heal others through your own suffering....

LONDON
17TH NOVEMBER, 1953

… I am enclosing a relic of Blessed Martin—I can't remember if I sent you one before. Do pray to him for yourself; he is *such* a lovely person, and just now obtaining wonderful and miraculous answers to prayer.…

11TH APRIL, 1954
PALM SUNDAY

… Now I am only writing to thank you for your letter and for the lovely little card for Clare (I will give it to her when I see her next week), and to say how overjoyed I am that you have been able to make a start. I admire you more than I can say, and I am convinced that God—and St. Thérèse—will go on helping you, and gradually—perhaps even suddenly—making it easier. One thing is important: if on some days you fail to keep your resolution about the diet (an excellent one, by the by), don't let that discourage you; remember that every mouthful you eat is a triumph and is building up your sanctification. If now and then you can't, it does not mean that all the grace and merit you have won by the times that you have succeeded are wiped out. No; if you have succeeded, say ten times, you are ten times stronger.

I have been praying for you every night and shall go on.

I will, as I say, answer you fully. But this is just to thank you for your letter—and for *yourself*, with all your courage and honesty, which is an inspiration to me.

You know, I had [an] absolutely *certain* intuition or conviction, or whatever you like to call it, just when I was saying goodbye to you, that you *are* going to triumph, and that your trials, and especially your victory over yourself, which is more than beginning, are not only going to sanctify you, but to save many other souls.…

XIII

A Note on Repentence

This is not an answer to your letter, but just a forerunner to say how deeply I sympathise. Of *course* I'm not shocked, "grieved," or anything else; given the *chance*, let alone the temptation, I would certainly have done the same thing over and over again—not once only, after years of *heroic* virtue! As the Rector told you in more delicate terms, everything comes out in the wash.

I shall write at length, tonight or tomorrow. This is only to say:

(a) I am impressed above all by your humility, your *great* love of God, shown by flying straight to His arms with a child's trust; and I am sure the whole thing will bring you—*has* brought you—floods of grace.

(b) In case of any future complications, you can depend on me for *any* kind of help, even to taking on the *whole* responsibility.

6TH APRIL, 1953

Thank you very much for your kind—much *too* kind—and generous letter. If I ever do anything to help you or anyone else (and I really can't think of anything concrete that I do!) it is only possible because I am so much a sinner that I understand well how even the slightest discouragement from outside oneself, added to the chronic close-on-despair inside, can crush one altogether, and *no* admonishing of virtuous people is ever of the slightest help—at least it is not to me. One doesn't want a preacher or even a shining example, but someone who will share the burden, even if they know they can't carry their own.

However, last night I was thinking for hours about what a lot of people I know who were deep in misery and confusion *last* Easter, but who have had the courage to accept their responsibilities and to accept life as it is, and who are now happy and have found real joy from accepting what looked like an insupportable burden... Then there is yourself, and at least the peace of being your own mistress (and I hope no one else's).

... I will write again in a few days, when the rush is over. Then I will reply to your question about the sins of the flesh. I expect you have forgotten it, but I have it in a letter of yours at the cottage, to which I return tomorrow.

The core of the answer, anyway, is that we sin against *God* in the first place, not against each other, though the latter may also be involved, and usually is. Actually, the protest that immorality "doesn't hurt anyone" is false; it almost certainly does. There is the lawful wife or husband who is betrayed and, if anyone concerned has children, they are almost certainly caused bitter suffering, though their parents may not realize it. But the worst thing is that these sins, that may seem "harmless" to us, deface and kill Christ in our soul, and *that* not only harms us ourselves, but harms *everyone* in the whole world....

XIV

A Note on Friendship

… I am up now, and the pneumonia is cleared up, but I admit I have never in my life felt more like something well chewed that the cat has brought in. But it's nice to be able to stay alone in my warm room and write: my work is behindhand and in chaos, so I hope for comparative solitude to get on with it. Unfortunately, however, people are now pestering to come and see me again, and some of them have. When they do come they all declare I look the picture of health, and obviously do not believe that I have had pneumonia at all! …

A very interesting and unusually nice Mohammedan, who has become very interested in Catholicism through reading *Guilt*, called on Saturday. He wanted a full and exhaustive exposition of the doctrine of the Blessed Trinity from me—a thing I find taxes every ounce of mental concentration at the best of times. I wished Frank or Maisie had been there. Anyhow, I was able to persuade him to read *Theology and Sanity*.

I am terribly glad that you are feeling more at peace and have found happiness in your two new friendships. But I feel that one tiny word of advice is needed. I am convinced that they both *are* as good and beautiful in character as you think, and from S.'s letter, enclosed, as well as from what you tell me, she is very wise too. But the warning is this: do not ask from any human being that which God only can give. I grant you that God gives Himself through human beings and unites Himself through human relationships, provided the people involved realize their human relationships as a mutual giving and receiving of Christ-life and the Holy Spirit, and do nothing to frustrate this. But God does not give Himself wholly through any *one* friend, lover, husband, or what not: I mean rather that although every real friendship is a mutual Christ-giving, no one friend can give God to you so perfectly as completely to satisfy and fill your need for His love.

Human elements enter into *every* human relationship, and disturb the serenity of them all sometimes. You see, we all tend to ask from the other human being things that God alone can give and we can only attain by a mutual and conscious turning to God together, and accepting from God together whatever suffering is the condition of love—and of course suffering in *some* measure is the condition of all love and every love. Take, for example, security, in the sense of being certain that nothing will ever come between oneself and the friend—that they will never be taken away. Well, one *knows* that to try and think so is sheer escapism; you, my dear, know it all too well. Every happy husband and wife *must* be secretly haunted, especially as they grow older, by the knowledge that one or the other will die first and the other will be left alone. No matter how many friends or children they have, no one will ever be able to fill the place in their soul of the one who has gone....

God's love for those we love is infinitely greater than our own, and it is as well to remember it, and to remember it especially when He allows things to happen which threaten both their happiness or safety, and ours.

And it is also the ultimate reason why, despite the Christ-giving element in our relationships, they can never be perfect here. There must be empty places left in our hearts, because the final happiness of both depends upon God Himself possessing us completely: once that is achieved, heaven can begin for both, and in heaven of course, unlike here, our friendships will take part, not only imperfectly, in God, but perfectly.

That, however, won't happen here; so, while thanking God for the joy and miracle of your new friendships, do not demand perfection of them, and do not be disappointed when trials arise. Actually, but for the failure of other relationships in your life, and for the suffering you have had through them, which by the by you have borne with magnificent fortitude and sweetness, but for those things you would not now be ready, fashioned as it were by the hammer of God, for these friendships....

XV

To Lucile Hasley

Caryll had much admired Lucile Hasley's writings in various periodicals, had been eager that Sheed and Ward should publish a collection of them, and had agreed to write an Introduction. Lucile on her side had become one of Caryll's most eager readers and had begun a correspondence carried on with great zest on both sides. One of Mrs. Hasley's letters Caryll kept, and the story is so interesting that I have included it in this collection.

819 Nell Gwynn House
27th May, 1948

... Regarding the conflict between the "Catholic Worker type" and the "Keep to the Middle of the Road"—what strikes me is that there ought not really to *be* any conflict, and that it is caused by a whole lot of mistakes which are generally accepted without question.

First of all, take the Catholic Worker type. You get papers from them, in which practically every article is a very vital grouse about injustice, and a few boosting up tbe worker as such, and they are usually illustrated either by a wood- or lino-cut of Our Lord or St. Joseph driving a huge nail into a splitting plank with a wooden mallet which would be ruined by the action. (Being a carver—in wood—by trade, this picture worries me.) But what is lacking in these papers is any articles that seem likely to make Christ more real to the worker himself in his own life, as if the only consideration is his just grievance, and the duty, shared by him with all men, to try to remedy it. What is absent is the suggestion of his being in unity with Our Lord in *suffering* injustice, or any real understanding of work itself, the integrity of the artist at work, which should be every worker's ideal, or the honour he has in practicing and suffering as Christ did, or the glory of being poor, and so on. Also it seems to be presumed that the rich man (a) doesn't work at all, (b) doesn't suffer any injustice at all. I could start pages on the superficial side of this, but don't want to get away from the heart of it—namely, that in the Mystical Body we are all one, and we do all experience the Passion in a thousand secret ways, and we share—if we want to or not—in each other's lives and responsibilities. When I read snob-stuff from "Catholic Action" people of the "Flame" type, and when I see it practiced, it turns my blood to poison; but I think the tendency to segregate *every* type and class, at least in the mind, leads to a vast number of individuals completely misunderstanding themselves and their own glory. If everyone was concentrating on being a "Christ" in and through his own circumstances as they are, then I think that inevitably all the injustices *would* be righted.

If I appear gentle—alas, I am not: I asked my dearest friend, with whom I live—she should know—and she said, "*I* don't think so." But *any* holding back there is at all in me is based on cowardice. I am a frightened, abject creature, (a) because in youth I was broken right across (psychologically!), early and irrevocably, so started pretty well defeated; and (b) because I really am a sinner and suffer a continual guilt (remorse which measures my vanity) and fear, not alone of being seen just as I am by those I love, but even of facing myself and seeing. So I do not dare to judge, though in private life I do even that, and am often sore and bleeding from the shame of the rash judgments I have made myself, and my indiscretions regarding them. But the older I grow, the more unwilling—and afraid—am I to preach. That's why I prefer writing fiction: it's more like a big gesture of sympathy—like taking hold of another sinner's hand and pressing it lovingly as we walk together, not seeing one another's face, down the same dark stinking passage in the same fetid prison.† When I write "spiritual" books now, it's for the reason that I know that many people will read them who won't read fiction (the reverse applies too): and I also want to give some sympathy to a lot of those; but believe me, the last one that I wrote, which is not yet published, I did literally write in tears.

This letter, by the bye, is from friend to friend. These are not the things I would fill up on a publicity "questionnaire"—but then I wouldn't fill up anything on them: I don't like intimate publicity at all.

I am very sure you aren't "suffering from lack of charity and spiritual pride"; you have, on the contrary, the splendid supernatural vitality of St. Paul, and it is a great gift to thank God for; I thank Him for it in you. I am sure you ought to go straight on, with your courage and wonder in the Faith driving you, and not to stop and question it at all....

I shall hope very much for more from you—not in fannery but in friendship.

(From Mrs. Hasley)

... We all share the Passion, as you say, in a thousand secret ways, and I would like to say that I, personally, have been to hell and back during this past month. On May 2nd my little girl made her First Communion and then, the next day, was stricken with rheumatic fever. On the afternoon of the same day, I received the result of my X-rays. I haven't been well since a trip south (Georgia) last August and I finally got the courage to investigate. The verdict of three doctors was this (sparing you the details, of course): "A grave and rare ailment for which there is no

---

† Prison of self: my life is happy and I have a nice one-room flat!

cure." There would be diet (eating only canned strained baby food) and there would be surgery, but neither would cure. Bluntly, I faced much suffering and a messy death, and I didn't know how much time I had.

… All I felt was sheer horror and panic. So scared I could neither eat nor sleep. Finally I fled to the priest at N.D. and wept on his shoulder. "No use to pray," I said. "To pray for me is to pray for a miracle." It so happened that this was a priest with guts. "Very well," said he in ringing tones, "we will pray for a miracle. *You* will have said 'Thy will be done': *I* have said it. Now let us organize a campaign of prayer."

I confess that I myself had no faith. I felt the prayers would bring me the grace of resignation eventually, that was all. Still, that was plenty and, since I needed gallons of grace to calm the gnawing FEAR in my stomach, I appealed to the highways and byways. I do have a Catholic following…lay and clerical…and I hit out in every direction. I appealed to priests who were indebted to me for free manuscripts and the response came back like bread upon the waters. I also appealed to editor priests who wouldn't want to lose a perfectly good contributor.… The typical touch was that, miserable as I was, I still felt abashed; I still hammed it up. I would write: "You are cordially invited to join a campaign for a miracle…the object of which, unfortunately, is me." The priests, however, said my disposition was no obstacle as long as I abandoned myself to God's will. This I did, for the main and simple reason that I had no choice in the matter. Believe me, *never* has heroic sanctity appealed to me so little. Just wanted to live. Four local priests (all personal friends of mine) really took things over. One promised an hour of Adoration *daily* (the busiest man on the campus); another, this or that penance; and each, of course, personally asked for prayers from those whom they considered close to God. In particular, a Brother Cosmas. He is a very holy Brother from Switzerland, and a mystic. They keep him under cover. He serves seven to eight Masses a day.

So, a week ago Tuesday…this is what happened. It just so happened that this was the day for a *de luxe* examination to see if there were, as yet, any perforations in the colon. (Ulcerative condition and closing of the colon were my trouble.) I was pea-green just thinking of it. So, on this morning I received a packet of dust from the grave of Blessed Martin, from my dear friend Ann Harrigan.... Well now, two months ago I wouldn't have swallowed the dust from anyone's grave but...you know...fear and helplessness have a way of dispelling sophistication. So, at *noon* I swallowed the dust (and my pride). At one o'clock, this N.D. priest met Brother Cosmas and said to him: "Brother, are you still praying for this woman?'" and the Brother replied: "*The prayers have been heard. She is all right.*" At 2.45 I went in for this examination, and the doctor, after a minute and gruelling examination, announced—baffled!—that I was organically sound, that I was all right, that I was even *dismissed*. I was simply dazed.

The priests, my husband, my friends, have accepted this without blinking an eye. I was next instructed to go back to the doctors and get as definite a statement as possible from them. The one was baffled and said rather surlily: "Who knows these things? Who knows?" The other one said: "Frankly, I was astounded. It is my sincere opinion that the evidence is all in favor of supernatural intervention.... "

... Can you believe this, or does it scandalize? I, as a convert, can only say it makes cold shivers run· up and down my spine... I cannot explain it on natural grounds. At the same time, I confess that my position is not an enviable one. I was instructed to tell the "right people"...i.e. those who would not scoff or be repelled.... Well, it is interesting to see the reactions. The priest (that busy one) who promised me a daily hour of adoration is now continuing it for his own good...says he cannot afford to quit now. Others feel a great thrill in thinking *their* prayers part of it. (And, of course, no one knows what turned the trick. I understand quality counts more than quantity, but I had both, if you ask me. I have wonderful friends.)

And after all these nice spiritual responses from my friends, what am I doing? Do not sneer, but I quit smoking a week ago; I can think of no greater "giving up," since I have been a chain smoker for years and years. All my little nerve ends are whimpering for their nicotine. But spiritually...well, I am a little scared. I think there may well be a price attached to this. In fact, I've had a sample already. As I told you, everyone has accepted this thing without batting a theological eye, *but* my two best friends cannot take it. They had the faith to pray for me, but not to accept it, once granted. I scandalized them by swallowing that dust. It embarrasses them; they prefer not to notice it. Very superstitious and all.…

(From Caryll Houselander)
24TH JUNE, 1948

Thank you very much for your letter with its wonderful story. Of course it interests me profoundly, and fills me with joy. Though I did not know of the tragedy and so could not join in the prayers for the miracle, I *am* in the chorus of thanksgiving. By the by, if you attribute it mainly to the intercession of Bl. Martin de Porres, whose grave dust you swallowed, is it not the first-class miracle wanted to canonize him? It seems to me to have all the marks of a first-class miracle, and may not this be God's glorious answer to your "second conversion"—to crown a Negro saint, using you for the sign of his sanctity?

I simply can't understand your friends taking scandal, or whatever it is that they have taken, about it. As regards the dust, since you didn't ask *them* to swallow it, they have no grievance. If you *had* asked me to, I would have swallowed a bucketful for you gladly—I'd have to swill it down with water, or preferably gin, for it must be a real physical feat to swallow dust—though as a small child I used to eat earth and dirt from the garden path. My nurse frequently said (I was fastidious at table), "You must eat a packet of dirt before you die": as I considered death, and heaven following purgatory, very desirable, and the eating of dirt, owing to Nurse's reiterated remark, as essential to salvation as baptism, I ate it as often as I could, but I remember it being difficult and often resulting in sickness!

But to return to the miracle. How can anyone take scandal over the dust, since Our Lord mixed up clay and spittle to put on the eyes of the blind man He cured? Over and over again He asked for, or made use of, some very small, humble, seemingly absurd and inadequate thing to work a miracle. That was His choice: why, since God doesn't change, should it be any different now?

Indeed I don't sneer over the smoking—I mean the not smoking. I know how fearful it can be, for I also was for years a chain smoker—used actually to stay up most of the night so as to go on smoking; and, apart from the physical necessity—or disease—it had become, I felt towards it as if it were a person, a friend, whom I'd betray, if I cut it out. I did give it up, and for months—even now, occasionally—felt a pang as if I had lost a dear person. Like you, I cut it off completely, in a day; I tried to be moderate, but I'm too weak to do things moderately, so I had to stop. It was hell for three weeks, then got easy. It's years ago since I had that last cigarette—about six months before the war. I was awfully glad I'd got it out of my system when the war came, as I was continually in First Aid Posts and Fire Fighting units (on roof tops—the latter—quite often) where we were strictly forbidden to smoke at all. This drove lots of people more crazy than bombs! And of course the nervous tension increased the desire for it. I'm certain God will be delighted at such a gesture of real gratitude.

There seems to me no possible interpretation of the story but a miracle: well, how can anyone fail to rejoice in it? Miracles happen, after all, for God's glory, and you *had* paid the price in the awful suffering that necessarily went before.

I do wholly agree with you that many little miracles happen daily, almost unnoticed; and there are many little saints, quite unnoticed, and who will not be canonized or recognized. It is they, in my mind, who are holding back the raging waters, not of mere temporal destruction (that may happen easily) but of damnation…

17TH AUGUST, 1949

… I also had in mind, as I would be bound to do, a strong and beautiful impression of *you* from your letters and what you have told me and may perhaps not even know about yourself, which I have come to know (yes, *know*, not imagine) from reading, re-reading and thinking about your letters to me—and from praying for you. I think one can really get to know people by praying for them, including dead people one never met, who may be in purgatory; and of course, quite certainly one can by praying *to* people in heaven—i.e. saints and children who died before the age of reason, therefore still in their baptismal innocence. During the war, one night we were in the midst of a long and exhausting air raid. Our London barrage had been going on for hours, German planes coming over, in batches of a hundred at a time, in relays all night, and the barrage, which meant a non-stop, ear-splitting thunder of gun-fire going all the time. I was in a hospital helping give First Aid to the wounded, and got sent to a ward where there were patients who had been operated on that day and so could not be moved down to the parts of the hospital considered a little more safe (i.e. the basement, where our Post was). I was told to go to the ward and keep those poor patients (who could not move an inch) from being afraid. On the way upstairs I realized that my mind was quite empty and that there was not one thought in it with which to reassure anyone—and in any case I had no doubt the hospital would fall on us in a few minutes!

Suddenly I became acutely and *unquestionably* conscious of the personality of a little child of three at my side—the child of a friend, whom I never knew, but of whom I had heard constantly from this friend, and to whom I had often prayed. It seemed that this tiny child directed me from heaven, filled my mind with things to say, and with things that were effective and did the trick! A day or two later I had a letter from the dead child's father, saying: "I heard the barrage even from here" (he was in a suburb outside London) "and when I realized what was going on, I went on my knees and prayed to Mary" (the child) "to stay with you all that night, and it was the anniversary of the night she died." ...

It is not humility and modesty that makes me avoid reviews which are not forced on me: it is funk. I am very conscious of the poor quality of my work, and equally conscious of the fact that I've *got* to say things in it; and I am always afraid of the critics discouraging me so much that

I shan't be able to write any more at all—or perhaps, more truly, that I shall write with even more sense of—well, I don't know what to say: I was going to say "shame," but it's not exactly that: it is more suffering. But let it be.

Try not to let yourself mind what critics say *at all*, either good or bad: most critics are not worth listening to, anyway, though sometimes they do teach one a few things. But I have been reading all the criticisms of Thomas Merton's book, *The Seven Storey Mountain*, and I am simply amazed to find that (in my view anyway), though they are all unanimous in praise, not one has any real or whole grasp of the author's meaning, and they miss fundamental points—the key points of the book—every time. This has made me realize that it is really very silly to put your trust in critics!

I have only read what was quoted in *The Trumpet* about *The Passion of the Infant Christ*—and one bit in a rather horrid little religious magazine here, which a friend sent to me, and which, though kindly intended, I think, says everything that I could possibly want not to have said about the book! ... I am going to write another letter to you—yes, I *really* am—very soon, in which I will tell you more about the very extraordinary circumstances which more or less *forced* me to write that book. But I need a little time to write that letter, and just at the moment I am doing everything against time. That's a mistake, I know; probably a sin against prudence too, and of course holy people insist that prudence is the "queen of the virtues." I doubt it, subject of course to correction; but if Prudence does hold that position, then I would prefer to discover a charwoman among virtues and to consort with her....

Your third question is: how I deal with correspondence. Well, it simply defeats me. I get letters from America, Canada, Australia, India, Africa, Holland, Germany, France, Switzerland, Hungary, Portugal, Spain—mostly from poor little people in real trouble of soul or body. Sheer fan mail I seldom answer, though I feel guilty, for I am really grateful to those who are kind enough to write it. But I try to answer the people who really do want help—and I just am never through. I have reduced myself to four hours' sleep in twenty-four, and still it is never done. To add to this dilemma, I work (under doctors) for neurotic and borderline people and in a mental hospital, and they, each one of them, expect my whole attention; they too write letters almost daily, and are fearfully offended if they are not answered....

By the by, there was one more question you wanted a reply to: how I earn my living. Just writing. The other things mentioned are all unpaid. I have had to give up all other paid jobs, except writing, so as to have time to do it in, and it's now harder than ever to get the time! I have done lots of other jobs, but I don't now—excepting (also not for pay now, though I used to do it for my living) wood-carving. I only want to carve crucifixes, and now and again a statue of Our Lady or a saint—but it's hard to find time, though there is no work on earth which in my mind is more soothing and healing than carving wood....

30TH OCTOBER, 1949

I have been, so to speak, sitting [holding] your hand for days—living with you, and being quite marvellously comforted and sustained by you—ever since your really strong and lovely book [*Reproachfully Yours*] arrived....

That book will do untold good, because it is not only full of really Christian love and faith and the heroism that always seems to go unnoticed with that; but it is so profoundly, deeply and gloriously human.

How I wish I had been able to read the whole of it *before*, instead of after, trying to write an Introduction for it! I would indeed have written one that was more adequate and would have made me feel less ashamed. I am proud in any case to have my name in your book—but ashamed that what I have written does not touch at all on the *best* things in your writing. Anyhow, I don't think it will do harm, because most people skip Introductions anyway, and a dip into the real text of the book, on any page at all, would make *anyone* buy it and read it.

Ever since I have had it, it so happens I have been more or less always shut up in my one-roomed flat with the baby already mentioned to you.... Judging from an article you sent me once, I presume that your Danny is three: well, Clare is two: your girls have also been two. You can therefore well imagine how it is to be in one room, with rain pouring down outside, precluding walks, and every so often a blanket of fog: no assistance, and a two-years-old girl—at the same time, writing against time! Life on these terms is further complicated by shopping and the necessity to eat, so pronounced in babies. Here, if you want to buy a loaf of bread, even, you've got to queue for it; meat or fish that isn't high has a queue miles long: as to bananas, I no longer try. Well, to manage these queues in pouring rain and fog, with a baby, just needs all the supernatural help there is from what source God will give it. Now, your book gives it. Little Clare has gone home for a week now, but now I can think of all the countless women who have to live their life in terms of reality, not in terms of so-called, but probably unreal, mysticism: and I rejoice, because after last week, in which your book brought me the most real strength and sense of worth-while-going-onness I have ever known, I realize that it will give the same to countless people of every sort, in as great and greater need....

I wish you would send me snaps of yourself and your children. They all fascinate me after reading your book. It really does get to the core of real life and real love.

Designed by Fiona Cecile Clarke, the Cluny Media *logo depicts a monk at work in the scriptorium, with a cat sitting at his feet.*

The monk represents our mission to emulate the invaluable contributions of the monks of Cluny in preserving the libraries of the West, our strivings to know and love the truth.

The cat at the monk's feet is Pangur Bán, from the eponymous Irish poem of the 9th century. The anonymous poet compares his scholarly pursuit of truth with the cat's happy hunting of mice. The depiction of Pangur Bán is an homage to the work of the monks of Irish monasteries and a sign of the joy we at Cluny take in our trade.

"Messe ocus Pangur Bán,
cechtar nathar fria saindan:
bíth a menmasam fri seilgg,
mu memna céin im saincheirdd."

Printed in Dunstable, United Kingdom